WINNIPEG

D0507080

NOW I KNOW WHY

TIGERS

EAT THEIR

YOUNG

NOW I KNOW WHY TIGERS EAT THEIR YOUNG

Surviving a new generation of teenagers

• third edition •

Dr. Peter Marshall

foreword by Barbara Coloroso

whitecap

Copyright © 2007 by Dr. Peter Marshall
Whitecap Books

All rights reserved. No part of this publication may be
reproduced, stored in a retrieval system, or transmitted
in any form or by any means, electronic, mechanical,
photocopying, recording or otherwise, without the prior
written permission of the publisher.

All recommendations are made without guarantee on the
part of the author or Whitecap Books Ltd. The author and
publisher disclaim any liability in connection with the use of
this information. For additional information, please contact
Whitecap Books, 351 Lynn Avenue, North Vancouver,
British Columbia, Canada V7J 2C4. Visit our website at
www.whitecap.ca.

Edited by Elaine Jones
Proofread by Ben D'Andrea
Design by Five Seventeen
Illustration by Tom Bagley

LIBRARY AND ARCHIVES CANADA CATALOGUING IN PUBLICATION

Marshall, Peter Graham, 1947–
    Now I know why tigers eat their young : surviving
    a new generation of teenagers / Peter Marshall.
    —Rev. and expanded.
ISBN-13: 978-1-55285-859-2
ISBN-10: 1-55285-859-6
    1. Parent and teenager.
    2. Parenting. I. Title.

HQ799.15.M37 2007   649'.125   C2006-904984-X

The publisher acknowledges the financial support of the
Government of Canada through the Book Publishing Industry
Development Program (BPIDP) and the Province of British
Columbia through the Book Publishing Tax Credit.

Printed and bound in Canada

To my cubs —

Aaron, Alexandra, Joanne, Kiera, and Tim.

With much love as well as my thanks
for making over three decades of parenting
so rewarding.

CONTENTS

FOREWORD

Parenting is a unique profession. What other demands such a high level of skill, commitment, and creativity while offering little, if any, training? In two decades parents are expected to take a newborn child and create a well-adjusted, independent, and responsible adult. They have to prepare their children to cope with the many challenges they'll encounter as they approach the teenage years; drug abuse, delinquency, sexual promiscuity, and depression are examples of the dangers and risks that exist for young people in our complex and stressful society.

The family itself faces its own challenges. After the upsurge of separation and divorce, the two-parent, nuclear family is no longer the norm. While single-parent families and stepfamilies can be very successful, they also place unique demands on parents' ingenuity and skill.

Throughout my professional career I've argued that there's no recipe for parenting. There's no tried-and-true collection of techniques for raising children, and there are no experts who can give parents the secrets of success. There are, however, ideas and approaches that can be explored. There are ways to foster self-esteem and opportunities to teach children the principles of responsibility and mutual respect. Parents have tremendous power to shape and strengthen the family. Using this power wisely becomes so important as children grow older: the teenage years require a delicate balance between the young person's need for independence and self-reliance and the parent's need for influence and authority.

Now I Know Why Tigers Eat Their Young reflects all of these values and perspectives. Dr. Marshall neither preaches nor prescribes; instead, he combines his personal and professional experiences in a way that parents will find thought-provoking, reassuring, and useful. Peter treats the subject matter with respect, but he also adds his personal brand of humor that makes the book as entertaining as it is informative.

This new edition includes content from the workshops Peter has been asked to give on many aspects of parenting. He has added a chapter on lifestyle, which addresses not only nutrition and exercise but also teenagers' growing concerns about the environment. The chapter on the benefits and dangers of the Internet is particularly timely given the media accounts of Internet stalking and luring. Peter provides information and suggestions that will be helpful to parents, even those with little familiarity with computers.

Above all, *Now I Know Why Tigers Eat Their Young* gives parents practical and thoughtful advice to help their teenagers grow into responsible, resourceful, and resilient people who treat themselves and others with dignity and regard.

—Barbara Coloroso
  educator and author of *kids are worth it! Giving Your Child the Gift of Inner Discipline, Parenting with Wit and Wisdom in Times of Chaos and Loss, The Bully, the Bullied and the Bystander,* and *Just Because It Isn't Wrong, Doesn't Make it Right*

CHAPTER 1

THE CHICKEN LITTLE SYNDROME

After more than 25 years in the business, I have to confess that I've never overcome my secret urge to be famous. I've finally realized that my only chance of standing next to the greats in the Psychology Hall of Fame is to discover something. So, just as Freud gave us the Oedipus complex and Jung introduced us to the collective unconscious, I've uncovered a new disorder—the Chicken Little Syndrome.

At the core of CLS (which is how it will be referred to after I become famous) is something I've labeled "sociological hypochondriasis." I picked this term because it meets the criteria for scientific respectability—it's totally incomprehensible and has more than five syllables per word. Like the physical hypochondriac for whom a mere twinge is sufficient cause to summon friends and loved ones to his bedside, the sociological hypochondriac looks at what is happening in society and immediately sees signs of decay and imminent disaster. Those stricken with this disorder have an absolute field day when it comes to teenagers. They look at young people's behavior and are convinced they have found proof positive that the sky is about to fall.

Many of those afflicted with CLS have a severe case of the GOD complex (Good Old Days complex). They're easy to detect because of their addiction to *Little House on the Prairie* reruns. They've come to believe that there really was a wonderful era when children always referred to adults as "sir" or "ma'am" and when their worst crimes were pilfering cookies, after which they were so guilt-ridden they confessed and insisted on being taken out to the woodshed for a licking.

My interest in CLS has turned me into a history fan. This amazes me as I'd always thought of my high school history teacher as nothing more than living proof that the capacity to be boring and irrelevant was a marketable skill. As a result of the exhaustive research I've undertaken over the past two days, I've found evidence that the belief that the upcoming generation will propel the rest of us into oblivion existed in antiquity. Over 2,000 years ago Socrates took a few moments out of the daily grind of figuring out the meaning of life to comment on the young people of his day: "Children today are tyrants: they contradict their parents, gobble their food, and terrorize their teachers." In the 18th century it was ministers who took on the task of assassinating the character of the younger generation. There's an account of a minister who warned parents that, "as innocent as children seem to be, they are young vipers. They are infinitely more hateful than vipers and are in a most miserable condition." If that wasn't enough to make the point, he wanted to ensure that children would eventually be given feedback regarding their miserable condition. He emphasized that they are "naturally senseless and stupid" and asked, "Why should we conceal the truth from them?"

One short description of children from that era is a particular favorite of mine. The person who referred to children as "curly, dimpled lunatics" may have been overstating his case, but I suspect he was a parent who was just having a particularly bad day and was viewing a childless marriage as a golden but missed opportunity.

No historical account would be complete without a quote from that noted expert on teenagers—my mother. It was not long after I had entered my teens when she looked me squarely in the eye and said, "Peter, there are many paths to hell, but why did you have to choose all of them?"

IT'S TIME FOR AN AUTOBIOGRAPHY

One of the best ways to combat CLS is to remember one's own past. Many parents, however, seem to suffer from retrograde amnesia. This is a fancy term for loss of memory. It's often used to describe what can happen to a person's memory after an accident or trauma. Having a child can, of course, be either or both. Retrograde simply means "before," and amnesia—I forget what this means. Parents of teenagers are particularly prone to this type of selective loss of memory. If I'm honest, however, I can still recall enough of my childhood to know that I wasn't born a pillar of society and that my behavior often posed a serious threat to my parents' sanity. "Me and the boys" found ways of entertaining ourselves that tested the limits of the criminal code. (I'd like to think that "me and the girls" carried on in much the same way, but I was singularly unsuccessful in this regard.)

Now, those of you who led blameless childhoods and never caused your parents one sleepless night should stop reading immediately. I invite the rest of you who haven't completely repressed your growing-up years to complete the following exercise. It has two parts. The first can be completed on your own. The second is shared with someone else. If you have a spouse, she or he could participate. If not, find someone of similar age who doesn't have a history of blackmail or extortion.

Part 1 is designed to stimulate your memory. Take pencil and paper and tackle the following questions:

1. Name two things you and your parents argued about regularly.
2. Were you ever lectured by your parents because of your performance at school—or lack of it?
3. What were five obscene words you knew and had used by the age of 15?
4. Did you ever go to, or hold, a party without your parents' permission?
5. At what age did you first try alcohol?

6. What music did you listen to and what did your parents think of it?
7. Did you ever hang out with friends that your parents disapproved of?
8. What best describes your room as a teenager:
    a. Suitable for a full-page spread in *Better Homes and Gardens*
    b. Borderline presentable
    c. Eligible to be declared a conservation area because of the rare forms of life flourishing in its corners
9. Did you ever steal in the community or from your parents? (Yes, "borrowing" from the change on the dresser counts unless you've paid the money back with interest.)
10. Name one job you were given by your parents that you knew was reasonable but complained about regularly.
11. Did you ever argue about use of the family car? Did you do anything to (or in) the car that upset your parents, or would have upset them if they had known about it?
12. Think of a time you lied or otherwise deceived your parents that they still don't know about. (I dare you to tell them now.)
13. Did you ever experiment with street drugs such as marijuana?
14. Did you ever look at pornographic magazines?
15. What is THE WORST THING you ever did as a teenager?

Part 2 is an exercise that is a great icebreaker at workshops. It's based on observing my wife when she's with her siblings and old high school friends. Kathy has two brothers and two sisters. Their father never read Benjamin Spock, and his definition of permissiveness was giving them the choice between bowing and saluting when he came home. They also went to a Catholic school, and in those days the nuns didn't fool around when it came to instilling knowledge and correct behavior in their charges. Talking en route to your next class was a venal sin, and any boy caught with his hands in his pockets was sent to the Grand Inquisitor. As a result, the children devoted much of their time and energy to finding ways to beat the system at home and school. Listening to them talk about what they got up to with one another or with their friends is quite an education. The best part of their reminiscing is observing my in-laws' reactions when they're treated to these trips down memory lane. As yet they have only been permitted to hear segments of the collective memoirs—you have to take such things very gently. At times they seem amused. On other occasions, however, they're clearly shocked. You can see signs of disapproval, and you know that if there were a way to ground a middle-aged son or daughter, they'd find it.

So sit down together with your lists and take turns talking about what you were like as teenagers. Try to outdo one another. You'll probably find that once your partner has disclosed a few of his or her misdemeanors it will feel safer to talk about your past with abandon. In no time at all it will be like you're being interviewed for a lead article in *True Confessions*.

LEARNING FROM EXPERIENCE

Sometimes it seems as if teenagers waste a lot of time discovering what we've known and have been trying to teach them for years. I've met parents who are open in discussing the problems they had themselves during their adolescence. Remembering their negative experiences makes them determined that their son or daughter won't make the same mistakes. I have no difficulty empathizing with them. The drive to protect our children and our wish that they not be hurt in any way are very strong. But I've come to appreciate that children can't always learn through hearing about other people's experiences. It simply doesn't work. This seems to be true at all stages of development.

One example with young children is the "lesson" of the importance of sharing. I recall one specific occasion when our youngest child, Alexandra, was playing with a friend's daughter. Both were toddlers. Tears and raw violence had erupted over possession of the favorite toy of the moment. Feeling the pressure to demonstrate my child-rearing skills, I offered suggestions about taking turns that were met with looks that, roughly translated, said, "Tell someone who cares." Fortunately, Alexandra eventually yawned, or at least opened her mouth wide enough that I could pretend she had. This permitted the lame but often-used justification for antisocial behavior: "She's a bit cranky, you know; she needs a nap."

Alexandra and Jennifer became good friends. As they grew older they discovered that sharing could help them have a lot of fun. When they wanted to play school they learned that, while they could do this on their own, cooperation allowed them to have both a teacher and a student who could act out imagined scenes. All this learning took place with very little teaching from their parents. Discussing abstract ideas such as sharing is unlikely to have much impact: children need to experience the negative consequences of not sharing and the positive consequences of working cooperatively.

The importance of learning through experience continues during middle childhood and adolescence, and I encourage parents to use their autobiographies as a means of recognizing how much they also learned through trial and error. I like to join in such discussions. We often agree that the bad choices we made helped us appreciate the need to be careful when it came to forming friendships. Some of our assertiveness may have developed only after having experienced how unpleasant it feels to allow yourself to be dominated or manipulated by others. Like several teenagers I've seen, I didn't understand the value of education until I discovered for myself that not having a high school diploma closed too many doors.

Wouldn't it be so much easier if they would simply listen and learn? If you're very lucky your daughter or son may be a highly reflective and open person who will consider, analyze, and then accept much of your advice. I've tried to get such a teenager, but I'm told they've been back-ordered for years. For most of us, learning through experience is necessary; it's also a powerful way of acquiring ideas and values, as it's based on real, rather than imagined, consequences.

REMEMBERING YOUR PAST AS AN ALTERNATIVE TO TRANQUILIZERS

One aspect of writing a biography that I find interesting is the comparison between myself as a teenager and how I am as a man in my fifties. Certainly there are some similarities, but the differences are more compelling. If I had presented a panel of experts with a profile of myself at 16 and asked for an objective opinion about my chances of becoming a reasonably stable and productive member of society, I'm doubtful I'd have been rated an odds-on favorite. In a similar vein, it's not uncommon for parents to tell me, "I know he'll turn out all right," but to say it in such a way that you know they're having a very hard time believing it.

This is where retrograde amnesia exerts such a strong influence. I can remember the outrage and fear elicited from many parents in the early sixties at the sight of the hippies and flower children. While I and many of my generation grew our hair below our ears, listened to the Beatles and Rolling Stones, and wrote poetry with no punctuation, our parents watched in horror, lamented our impending doom, and thought, "There goes the human race." Somehow we survived reasonably well.

I have to acknowledge this optimistic view isn't held by all. It can be argued that things are indeed different today; the fact the previous generation turned out reasonably well is no guarantee the present one will enjoy the same fate. Dr. Spock, who wrote the most successful childcare book of all time, became sadly disillusioned about the younger generation shortly before his death. Looking at what he saw as the negative trends in society, he lamented, "Tote it up and you have a picture of a society speeding downhill." I will devote the next chapter to an attempt to convince you that today's generation of teenagers isn't on such an ominous path.

CHAPTER 2

WHAT'S THE MATTER WITH KIDS TODAY?

The fact that successive generations have expressed similar concerns about the youth of the day doesn't, of course, imply that these concerns always lack substance. But we need to be aware that teenagers have traditionally received a great deal of bad press. This can create a biased and negative picture of what they're really like. I won't attempt to provide a complete profile of teenagers today. I would, however, like to discuss some of the major concerns that have been expressed and draw heavily on the "looking back" approach of the previous chapter.

SEX

As a teenager I was led to believe that I was in the middle of a sexual revolution. I spent most of my adolescence trying to find out where it was being held and how I could sign up. In the eighties I heard the revolution was over and was left feeling I'd forever missed the chance to be part of history-in-the-making.

But did the revolution really happen? The answer seems to be "yes" and "no." It depends on what area of sexuality is being studied. It does appear that attitudes have changed; for example, there is greater acceptance of premarital sex now than was the case in the fifties. The notion that premarital sex is more acceptable for males than females is also less popular. This double standard was extremely strong in the past.

Changes in attitudes don't necessarily mean changes in behavior. Are adolescents more liberal or permissive when it comes to actually engaging in sexual behavior? This isn't an easy question to answer accurately. First of all, how can you be sure that adolescents (or adults) will answer questions regarding their sex lives truthfully? For example, when premarital sex tended to be frowned upon, adolescents might not want to admit to any experience with intercourse. When the social climate changed, perhaps they then felt reluctant to reveal their virginity. And that's only the start of the problems. You have to be sure adolescents know what you're asking. One researcher found that teenagers don't always understand common terms; one of the definitions given for losing virginity was "masturbating to a climax." Another teenager thought sexual intercourse was no more than socializing with the opposite sex. It's also hard to do truly representative research: findings that relate to African-American college students in New York don't necessarily apply to Caucasian high school graduates in Alberta.

So, what do we know? It seems safe to conclude that premarital sexual intercourse is more prevalent today than it was before the seventies, as are both "light" and "heavy" petting. Most of the increase, however, appears to result from the declining influence of the double standard. In the fifties and sixties less than one-third of girls had intercourse before the age of 19; now over half are sexually active with boyfriends. For boys the statistic has remained fairly constant at around 70 percent, although some researchers feel a slight increase may have occurred.

In spite of all the difficulties facing researchers in this area, there are indications that while there has been a "revolution," it's probably less dramatic than many of us think. Adolescents themselves typically overestimate how sexually active their generation has become. For example, if you ask teenagers what they think *other* teenagers are doing, you'll soon believe virgins are an endangered species. And, once again, you have to be careful when it comes to the statistics.

While they can be very useful in helping us understand behavioral trends, they can be misleading if used too selectively. For example, if I took the statistics for 19-year-old girls over the past few decades I could proclaim, "Researchers find a 200 percent increase in teenage sex." Now that's revolutionary talk. I could also justify the headline, "Most 17-year-old-girls are virgins—and they're still happy."

The statistics relating to behavior don't always tell us enough about how responsible teenagers are when it comes to sexual relationships. Parents may hope their teens abstain altogether; if this isn't the case, it can be reassuring to know they tend to be more knowledgeable about matters such as birth control and sexually transmitted diseases, as well as more willing to apply this knowledge in the form of safer sexual practices.

I also find it interesting to look at research that has examined the values teenagers have when it comes to being sexually active. It seems that while most teens will say premarital sexual intercourse is acceptable, they don't typically condone casual sex. To the contrary, most will say that other aspects of relationships are far more important, such as finding a girlfriend or boyfriend who is trustworthy, loyal, sensitive, and caring. Within the context of such a relationship they *may* say sexual intercourse is an option, but not a priority. In some ways it seems their values may, in fact, have more depth than those of their parents. One study asked teens and parents to rate different aspects of personality and appearance in terms of how desirable each would be in a dating partner. The teens certainly ranked physical attractiveness highly, but they gave greater priority to the characteristics mentioned above, such as sensitivity and trustworthiness. The parents, on the other hand, gave their highest rankings to superficial characteristics, such as manners, physical appearance, and conversational skills. This study helped me to understand one of the likely reasons for my lack of success on the dating scene in my youth. Obviously it was the parents who had made it known to their daughters that I was on the forbidden list; if I'd been a clean-cut, smooth-talking psychopath, however, they'd have loved me.

DRUGS

I came across a headline recently: "One in two youth still abuse drugs." That's obviously alarming and would make most parents very anxious about letting their children out of their sight, particularly if they were also aware of the statistics that tell us the majority of older students report drugs are readily available at school. I've taken the opportunity to reproduce the results of this study many times when I'm presenting to audiences on this topic. Imagine you're a subject in a similar study. First of all I tell you that abuse of drugs means having used an illegal or street drug at least once in your life. So if you so much as had one puff of a marijuana cigarette as a teenager—and even if you didn't inhale—you meet the criterion for drug abuse. I also remind you that alcohol is a drug, which means that a sip of wine, beer, or liquor gets you counted. I then ask you to raise your hand if you qualify as one of the young people who "still abuse drugs."

That headline is an excellent example of why it's important to remember Mark Twain's comment: "There are lies, damn lies, and statistics." Bad news sells, and statistics are easy to use in such a way as to suggest that the news is far worse than it is. In fact, although I've never attempted to count the show of hands when I conduct this survey with audiences, I'm sure I've never failed to top 50 percent. The only time I can recall less than that was at a school graduation. In this instance the results were undoubtedly influenced by the fact that the audience of parents was being watched intensely by the graduating students at the front of the auditorium.

I always emphasize that I'm not attempting to dismiss parents' concerns about drugs and alcohol. I work in settings where we struggle to help young people and their families deal with the damage caused by problems with addictions. But it's also important to recognize that the teenagers of today are less likely to experiment with drugs than their parents were when they were a similar age. While we have a long way to go, we have somehow managed to raise a generation of young people better able to say no.

MUSIC

After sex and drugs, it seems only fitting to move on to rock and roll. Our society seems to frown on almost all forms of censorship. One example is the morbid, sexual, and violent content of the lyrics in popular music. This is a topic I've heard many parents raise over recent years. Their concerns are two-fold. The first is that the lyrics might reflect the way young people are thinking and, as such, might be symptoms of emotional difficulties or a lack of moral standards. The second is that, even if listeners are well adjusted to begin with, listening to the music will warp their thinking and values.

I recall driving with my son and his friends to a swim meet. I'd lost the battle of the radio station; somehow I couldn't convince most of the occupants that listening to a full-length broadcast of a Gilbert and Sullivan operetta would make the miles just slip by. As I was listening to their choice of what they assured me was music, I had a nagging feeling the lyrics were less than appropriate for their tender years. I asked Aaron and his friends to translate, having promised that I wouldn't get angry and wouldn't make them change the station. Part of the song was as follows: "You're a shot-gun—*bang*! What's up with that thang?/I wanna know how does it hang?/Straight up, wait up, hold up, Mr. Lover./Like Prince said you're a sexy mutha—./Well-a, I like 'em real wild, B-boy style by the mile." I still haven't got a clue what the lyrics mean, but I know I should thoroughly disapprove.

A few days later I went into a record store and asked the young woman behind the counter to find the most disgusting, tasteless CDs they had, emphasizing, of course, that my interest was solely for research purposes. She was most helpful and talked about the discs that irate parents would return to the store on a regular basis. I forget all the titles, but "Sir Psycho Sexy" and "Suck My Kiss" come to mind. Another was "Me So Horny," as if we're supposed to care.

But are things that different from when we were growing up? I remember sitting in a family restaurant with Kathy and the children. As is usually the case, there was the kind of background music people may enjoy, but rarely pay attention to. For some reason I just happened to listen to the lyrics of one of the songs. This is the advice that Bob Dylan offered back in the sixties: "Everybody must get stoned." The same era brought us the Beatles. Their *Sgt. Pepper's* album became a classic in the pop world. Most people have probably heard the first track many times—"Lucy in the Sky with Diamonds." If you were a nerd—and I'm sorry if this proves to be a moment of truth for some of you—you thought the song was about someone called Lucy who just happened to be up in the sky with a bunch of diamonds, which, of course, is an obvious topic for a song. If, however, you were cool, you immediately knew the song was about LSD. A few years later on their double white album the Fab Four posed the question: "Why don't we do it in the road?" I can think of many reasons, but they felt the need to ask anyway. And what about Chuck Berry's request: "My ding-aling, my ding-aling. I want you to play with my ding-aling." If that generation of parents had followed the suggestions in the lyrics of their music, the world would have turned into a global Woodstock.

But, it is argued, what about the lyrics that seem to condone violence, including violence against women? Let me give you an example. This song portrays a young man who is offering advice to his girlfriend. The problem is she no longer wants to be his girlfriend and he's less than happy about the situation. He tells her: "Well, you know that I'm a wicked guy/and I was born with a jealous mind./And I can't spend my whole life tryin'/just to make you toe the line. . . . Let this be a sermon,/I mean everything I've said./Baby, I'm determined/that I'd rather see you dead." That's about as violent as you can get, but the song isn't recent. It was recorded by the Beatles on their *Rubber Soul* album in 1965. If you didn't recognize the lyrics, you'd probably recognize the song if you heard it. It's a catchy, upbeat number called "Run for Your Life." I suspect most people who know this song never truly listened to the lyrics; I also doubt that those who did were influenced by them.

Jeffrey Arnett at the University of Missouri conducted a study also supporting the notion that the music young people listen to is unlikely to influence how they act. He examined the relationship between teenagers' preferences in music and a wide range of behavioral measures. He was particularly interested in whether or not certain types of music were associated with tendencies to be impulsive and reckless. His results led him to conclude there was no causal connection between musical preferences and behavior. Similar findings have also been reported with young adults.

I'd never argue that parents should be indifferent to the type of music teenagers listen to—parents will decide for themselves what they consider offensive and unacceptable, be it in the form of lyrics, television programs, movies, or literature. For some families, active censorship is their way of making a very clear statement about moral standards and values. There's some reassurance, however, in knowing that it's unlikely the material young people are frequently exposed to is a serious threat to the values and behaviors parents have worked hard to instill in their children.

EDUCATION

When he described our educational system as one "that spews out children with no skills, no goals, no preparation for productive, satisfying lives," Dr. Spock must have wondered what the students were actually doing with their time for the 10 or more years they spent at school. A recent article in a national newsmagazine echoed Spock's condemnation. A parent was quoted as saying, "You start to feel that your child is a computer into which the school has placed a stupidity virus."

One recent survey in North America indicated a sizable number of parents today would agree that the quality of the education system has declined. We're told about high dropout rates; there's no doubt that failing to graduate from high school does lower the chances of finding employment, as well as restrict the range of opportunities open to young people in the work force. There are enough data, however, to conclude that the message "get your education first" has been heard and heeded by more teenagers than was the case for previous generations. In the 1940s only about half of the student body made it to graduation. At the beginning of the 1990s Statistics Canada tells us the dropout rate was 17 percent; it had fallen to just below 10 percent in 2005, which is similar to the rate in the United States. Boys, it seems, are more likely to drop out; a common reason is their desire to have a job and money.

Others would have us believe that the failure to teach the "basics" has led to a generation of young people who can barely get through an Archie comic book. When you begin to look at the situation more closely, however, signs of the Chicken Little Syndrome begin to emerge. Let me start with one of those quotes from history. This is how a national study group described students in 1950: "Unable to express ideas, either orally or in writing in lucid, accurate and fluent English." In spite of their rampant ignorance, this was the generation that went on to pioneer dramatic advancements in areas such as medicine, technology, and communications over the past few decades. Literacy rates appear to be higher among young adults than they were in their parents' day, and the percentage of students who complete postsecondary education has risen. Literacy rates in North America also compare favorably with those from around the world. The most recent United Nations Development Report is encouraging; along with other nations such as Japan, Sweden, Australia, and the United Kingdom, literacy rates in North America are the highest in the world.

There's always the danger of being seen as painting too rosy a picture. I have no doubt there's plenty of room for improvement in our educational system, just as there is in any field. I've come to believe, however, that the task is one of going from strength to strength rather than a desperate attempt to fight an epidemic of the stupidity virus.

YOUTH CULTURE AND THE GENERATION GAP

The notion of a "youth culture" has been used to describe one way in which adolescents attempt to establish separate identities for themselves. The assumption is often made that the values, beliefs, and priorities teenagers take on are very different from those of adults, resulting in a generation gap. The term "gap" also adds the idea that the separation between teenagers and parents is the result of irreconcilable differences: we don't understand them and they don't understand us.

How real is the generation gap? Sometimes it can seem like teenagers have become aliens. The way they look, speak, and act can seem incomprehensible in light of the fact that you've shared the same gene pool and home environment. When you consider their tastes in music, dress, hairstyles, and vocabulary, it seems impossible to escape the conclusion they must be under the influence of outside forces. Yet in other respects there may be less of a gap today than in the past. The sixties did bring a certain counterculture, with groups of young people subscribing to ideas that were clearly at odds with those of the establishment, such as use of psychedelic drugs, commune-style living, and free love. But more recently there has been far less evidence that parents and teens differ with respect to their value systems. One way of studying this matter is to look at the sources of advice and potential influence adolescents turn to when making decisions. Do they sit at our feet ready to catch the pearls of wisdom we cast in their direction or do they seek counsel from their friends in the belief that we're out of touch, old-fashioned, and otherwise irrelevant?

The results of the research are mixed. Where adolescents look for advice depends very much on what particular matter is being decided. Let's start off with areas in which we're defunct. When it comes to questions such as dress, other aspects of personal appearance, choice of recreational activities, and appropriate hours of sleeping, we lack credibility in their eyes. I can live with this. In fact, there have been periods when I wanted this fact to be advertised: when Joanne and Tim were teenagers I had absolutely no wish to be seen as having any responsibility for the way they looked at times. But what about other areas of decision-making? When adolescents are presented with problems regarding money, education, or career plans, it seems they typically attach more importance to parents' opinions than those offered by friends. Furthermore, other research has failed to find the differences between young people's values and those of their parents that would be expected if there were truly a large generation gap or distinct youth culture. When issues such as drugs, education, work, and relationships are explored, the attitudes held by adolescents and parents tend to be similar, and certainly more so than was the case in the seventies.

SO WHAT *IS* THE MATTER WITH KIDS TODAY?

There will be many issues and risks for each new generation of parents to consider and confront. As parents we share concerns about violence among young people. We know the dangers associated with alcohol, drugs, and early sexual activity and can only hope we have prepared our teens sufficiently to make good decisions. But I find some comfort in realizing there are many indications we've been successful in raising a generation of bright young people who typically have the values needed to make responsible decisions.

There's another side to the "good news." If there are positive and healthy trends among young people, we must have been doing something right. For example, why are most young people able to say no to drugs in spite of their greater availability? Presumably, if we can determine what underlies the positive trends, we'll be in a better position to tackle new problems as they arise. I'll return to this point several times throughout the book. For now, however, I'd like to offer my opinion that there really isn't that much the matter with teenagers today. The worst fears of preceding generations of parents didn't materialize. The fact that their offspring more than survived makes me optimistic ours will as well. It also encourages me to have a more positive view of the present than is often presented in today's media and childcare literature. The sky hasn't fallen, and I feel no urge to sell all my earthly possessions and perch on top of a mountain waiting for it to do so.

CHAPTER 3

GROWTH AND DEVELOPMENT

WHO INVENTED TEENAGERS ANYWAY?

It came as a surprise to me to learn that teenagers as we know and love them today didn't always exist. I've wondered if this is what my grandmother meant when she reminded us that things were better in the "good old days." Like most of us, I've always seen teenagers as being in a separate stage of development—truly in a class all their own. Before the middle of the 18th century, however, a very different view prevailed. Children, let alone teenagers, were not seen as a distinct group. They were viewed as mini-adults who were expected to behave as such as soon as possible. For example, crawling wasn't seen as the milestone it is today. Rather, the sight of one's offspring crawling on the floor was more likely to be viewed as animal-like behavior that should be promptly corrected. Special clothes were even designed that kept children in a rigid, adult-like posture as soon as they could stand.

Children did, in fact, function as mini-adults. Until the advent of child labor laws, which mostly came into effect in the latter part of the 19th century, children who in our day and age would be attending kindergarten could be employed full-time. Today child labor may be seen as exploitation, but not that long ago many families simply couldn't afford to support their children. Sons and daughters were needed to work in the home or had to contribute the meager earnings they could obtain from outside employment. Even very young children were more likely to be employed than schooled. Today, a three-year-old who can remember to hang up her coat, take her dishes to the sink, and flush—all on the same day—is applauded. Two hundred years ago the same child could have been employed as a bird scarer or goose girl on a farm, while her six-year-old brother was putting in 14-hour shifts at the local mill or underground mine. In the London of Dickens's time they might be washing bottles, sweeping chimneys, working the land, or employed as domestic servants.

In many respects the roles of these young people couldn't be distinguished from those of their parents. It must have seemed quite a formidable task to take a newborn child and have him or her ready for the working world in as few as five or six years. Given the short period of time allotted to create a fully functional mini-adult, it would have been hard not to have a generally intolerant attitude toward the inevitable childish behaviors of one's offspring. Because they were seen as deviating so much from the model of adulthood, young children were often viewed very negatively. A common belief was that they were basically bad and in need of very strict discipline in order to bring them into line quickly.

I love reading authors who wrote about children during the past few centuries. One writer, Samuel Springer, stated with conviction: "All children have wicked hearts when they are born. Even little infants that appear so innocent and pretty are God's little enemies." This quote came to mind when I was looking through the glass screen at the nursery in the maternity ward where my last child was born. Viewing times usually bring a steady stream of onlookers and admirers who comment with pleasure and affection about the little bundles. Alexandra was, of course, the most adorable and angelic of the bunch, but I had to concede that none looked as if they posed a significant threat to society. I began wondering, however, about how Sam would have reacted if he had been there. I had a picture of him breaking into a cold sweat at the sight of the Satanic hoard and urging us to see beyond their sweet expressions into the evil of their hearts.

The notion that children should be seen as qualitatively different from adults began to gain ground in the 19th century. Writers started talking about childhood as a distinct stage of development. This was an important shift; once you start recognizing that children have different capabilities and needs, you become less inclined to refer to them as God's little enemies when they don't behave like adults. Furthermore, by the turn of the century childhood was being divided into separate stages, and the concept of adolescence was born.

The shifts in thinking that occurred in society weren't just the result of idle speculation or armchair theorizing. Probably a major reason for separating adolescence from childhood and adulthood was the industrial revolution. One spinoff had been a rapid decrease in the need for child labor and, before too long, more and more young people were staying in school rather than joining the work force. As a result, people began to see the teenage years as a phase during which the adolescent was being gradually prepared to meet the demands of the adult world.

Adolescence wasn't "invented" until the turn of this century. I'll give you the name of the person responsible, but just in case you're thinking of banding together and initiating a class action suit, he's no longer around to face the consequences of his actions. Dr. Stanley Hall died almost 70 years ago. A prominent psychologist, he devoted two volumes to the stage of adolescence, which he saw as beginning at roughly the age of 12 and continuing into the early twenties. He wrote about many aspects of development in this stage. He covered topics such as physical changes, adolescent love, and intellectual development. In case you're wondering why he needed two volumes to discuss adolescence, he decided to include a section on "juvenile faults." I'm sure you can appreciate that it would have been hard to stop writing once he got going on this one.

Adolescence as a stage has remained part of society's thinking throughout the 20th century. Our expectations regarding adolescents, however, have changed dramatically. The early view was primarily that they were to be molded; they should be like sponges, soaking up the truth and wisdom imparted by adults. However appealing this philosophy might be, it didn't seem to catch on with teenagers; they've insisted on having their own culture and identity. In recent years, for example, teenagers have become one of the most important consumer groups, and market researchers carefully study their tastes, interests, and preferences. They have their own fashions, music, and literature. They also have a political identity, and there have been eras, such as during the Vietnam war, when they've become loud and powerful voices for change.

It made good sense to extend the period allowed for young people to develop. In our highly literate, industrial, and technological world it takes much longer to become educated. An obvious consequence is that the period of dependency on parents has increased. So have the demands on parents to take responsibility for assisting their children through this lengthy transitional phase during which so many important changes occur.

PHYSICAL GROWTH

The pituitary gland has a lot to answer for. It's no bigger than a pea, but it packs a punch to be reckoned with. Known as a "master gland," it gets the other glands going, secreting the hormones that are either directly or indirectly responsible for many of the changes that occur in adolescence. And unfortunately you can't check your kids in to have it taken out, like you can tonsils when they become troublesome. It's tucked away at the base of the brain, well hidden and protected.

Many changes occur in the body during adolescence. One of the most obvious is the rapid increase in height, referred to as the growth spurt. Weight also increases, as does the amount of both fatty and muscle tissue. You now find yourself looking at a son or daughter who has lost that childlike appearance and has very quickly acquired an unmistakably adult build.

Major changes take place in the brain. One statistic I love is that adolescent brains use only half the energy of those belonging to younger children. I used this fact to convince my teenagers they were dealing with only half a deck. (I confess I never gave them the full story. The drop in energy consumption continues throughout adulthood, but I saw no reason to overwhelm them with information.)

The sex glands and reproductive organs are another target for growth and development. These aspects of maturation form the period we know as puberty, which is discussed in the chapter on sexuality.

Several aspects of physical development have particular relevance for adolescents psychologically. While the glands and hormones responsible for the changes seem to get the job done eventually, they don't coordinate their efforts very well. The term "asynchrony" is often used here. It refers to the fact that growth in different parts of the body doesn't proceed at a consistent, uniform pace. One illustration is the very rapid increase in the size of the hands and feet. For a number of teenagers it's almost as if they've woken up one morning to find their limbs have become longer. During the period that the brain and the rest of the body are learning how to adjust to having longer limbs, the teenager will seem to be clumsy and gangly and will go through a period in which he is well-advised to stay away from china stores and take a temporary break from tap-dancing classes. Not surprisingly, rapid and uneven growth makes many adolescents feel awkward and self-conscious.

It's also established that the process of physical maturation begins at an earlier age than was the case in previous centuries. Although the reasons for this aren't known for sure, improvement in nutrition and health care may well be a major factor. This leaves us with two trends that are in exactly opposite directions. At the same time that society is prolonging adolescence, nature is speeding up the process of becoming physically mature. As a result we have young people whom we view very much as children who often see themselves as far more grown-up and mature than we do.

There has been interest in studying the impact of the age of onset of physical maturation. While it's typically earlier than in previous generations, it varies a great deal from child to child. For boys, early onset of physical maturation is a plus. Being successful athletically still offers greater status for boys than girls, and having their bodies mature will often give them an advantage in competitive sport. In comparison to late developers, the early bloomers are also more likely to be seen as attractive to girls and are in a better position to be selected for leadership roles. For their peers whose hormones aren't so quick off the mark, life can be more frustrating. They're often seen as generally less mature and less able to take on adult-like responsibilities. They're also more likely to see themselves negatively and, perhaps as a means of compensating for these feelings of inadequacy, can become rebellious and noncompliant. (A word of caution. If you have a 12-year-old son, don't start slipping growth hormones into his orange juice just because he hasn't started shaving. While it's true that late developers tend to find adolescence more frustrating, they typically survive just fine. Many other factors are relevant here. A late bloomer who has a supportive family and has established a circle of close friends won't suffer that much, even if he has to endure periods of ribbing in the changing room.)

For girls, the situation is more complicated. Early maturation is generally a disadvantage in the younger age group. Girls who are well into puberty in grade six or sooner often feel very self-conscious and are embarrassed by their precocious development. They're also likely to lack the maturity needed to cope with the unwanted attention they may attract. By grade seven or eight, however, being physically mature offers definite prestige, and it's the late developer who is more dissatisfied with her body and is likely to be experiencing anxiety and self-doubt related to lack of development.

Bodily changes have a substantial impact on the adolescent's self-concept. Girls worry about the shape and size of their breasts and become particularly concerned about their facial characteristics, skin, and hair. Boys tend to be preoccupied with the size and strength of their bodies. The increase in penis size is also a very important matter for them.

Once again, sex differences emerge. Overall, adolescent girls experience greater dissatisfaction regarding their bodies; this, we assume, is a product of the stereotyping that has conditioned girls to place excessive value on their physical appearance. In one study students were asked to rate both the attractiveness and effectiveness of their bodies. The girls who rated their bodies as being more attractive to others were found to have more positive self-concepts. Boys were different. It was the perceived effectiveness of their bodies more than physical attractiveness that was associated with greater self-esteem.

I'm reminded that, even though my adolescence was far from being the most content and settled period of my life, I was lucky in many respects. I think my hormones were a bit on the heavy side. I quickly developed hairy legs but never needed the fingers of both hands to count the hairs on my chest. As it happened, this wasn't a problem. I was in the school pipe band and every Friday I wore my kilt, my legs proudly displaying the proof of my emerging manhood. Still, I can remember how often we discussed and worried about the relative status of our physical development. We wanted our voices to break, boasted about an increase in shoe size, and scoured our faces for any sign of growth that would justify the purchase of a razor.

Wonderful though it might be, I'd like to see some design changes in the human body. If I'd been consulted I'd have recommended a far more gradual period of change. I'd also have insisted on not having the broad range of differences between children in the onset and pace of adolescence. After all, in many areas we routinely group children quite rigidly on the basis of chronological age. The school system is one obvious example. My wife teaches grades seven and eight and knows only too well the problems associated with having a group that, while consisting of young people of similar age, contains some who physically resemble young children and others who are capable of having children of their own. The speed and variability of physical growth and development may not present major difficulties for all adolescents, but for some they can create a period of insecurity and self-doubt.

THE AGE OF REASON?

This is the dangerous part of the chapter. There's a risk that any credibility I may have gained is about to be totally lost and that you'll be convinced psychologists should stick to running rats through mazes. One of the most important and dramatic changes in adolescents is that they become capable of sophisticated and rational thinking. While I'm the first to acknowledge it may seem sometimes that teenagers have left, rather than entered, an age of reason, I assure you this isn't the case. I'll also try to convince you that much of the insecurity and conflict that can be experienced by teenagers is, in fact, the result of their ability to think in different and more complex ways.

Take moral development, for example. Very young children have a notion of good or bad that's determined largely by external rewards and punishments rather than any internal moral code. They're very quick to recognize how people react to their behavior, and sensing disapproval can be sufficient punishment. At this stage, however, something is bad because it leads to a negative consequence, not because they feel it's basically wrong. As they get older, children internalize rules and standards—usually those of their parents and other important people in their lives. This acceptance isn't, however, based on any thinking about underlying moral or ethical principles; the children simply adopt the prevailing party line.

When you develop the capacity to think in more complex terms you can focus on the principles and ideas underlying a particular rule. For example, children may have been taught that it's wrong to hit other people. They'll automatically apply this principle and will see behavior such as bullying in the schoolyard as bad. As adolescents, they may begin to examine the more abstract idea that it's morally wrong to use physical force to solve problems. This can make life more complicated. If bullying is unacceptable because force is being used to dominate other children, why is it all right for societies to have armed military and police forces? Debating this and other issues can lead teenagers to doubt, question, and challenge many of the ideas and beliefs they have held.

The same capacity for complex reasoning will influence the development of other areas of life. One psychologist, Joseph Adelson, devised an interesting approach to studying political thinking. He asked subjects in his studies to imagine that a group of 1,000 people bought an island. The task was then to describe how this new society should be organized. He found that, unlike younger children, adolescents demonstrated an understanding of broad concepts, such as justice and equality, which they applied when creating their island society.

Earlier in this chapter, I briefly touched on the role of adolescents as a political force in our society. This was clearly evident in the sixties when the peace movement gained momentum in many parts of the world. While the current generation may not have such a high profile politically, I wouldn't underestimate its power and influence. Teenagers' interest in the environment provides an illustration. Every so often we hear reports of high school groups pressuring the catering companies to eliminate unnecessary packaging and disposable cutlery and provide recycling bins. Discussions about plastic knives and forks and pop cans may be less newsworthy than debates on the arms race, but like many others, I've come to believe that young people's developing concerns about how individuals and societies treat the environment are critical to ensuring our future welfare.

Religious values are also likely to be influenced by the changes in thinking capacity. Once again, the process is often one of questioning—of not automatically assuming that a viewpoint is correct simply because you've been brought up with it. The adolescent can become acutely aware of how many people subscribe to quite different religious beliefs and can find it an interesting intellectual endeavor to compare philosophies.

I devote a whole chapter of this book to self-esteem, as it's such a critical aspect of adolescent development. Just as teenagers can engage in more sophisticated thinking about the outside world, so their thinking about themselves can show greater range and depth. They start considering what it would be like to have different personalities. For example, a teenager may wonder whether or not she should be more assertive. She's able to imagine a variety of situations involving herself and others and weigh the pros and cons of being more assertive. If she decides the outcome would be favorable, she may decide to change her personality in this way.

The process of deciding the kind of person they want to be leads to the development of the ideal self. Creating this ideal version is important as it provides a goal to strive for. It can also be frustrating. It's like trying to keep New Year's resolutions. Most of us have to renew these annually: our attempts at self-improvement rarely last beyond mid-February. Inevitably, therefore, there will be a discrepancy between the ideal self and the real self.

After many years of living with them, I've become accustomed to my imperfections. I've also had the benefit of loved ones who, while not shy about reminding me of my shortcomings, display remarkable tolerance for them. As a result, my ideal and real selves seem to get along quite well, in spite of their differences. In early adolescence, however, the task of living with different versions of the self can become a major struggle. For example, our teenager with the goal of being more assertive may become very frustrated when she finds out how hard it can be to stand up for what she thinks and wants. For many young adolescents, this conflict between who they are and who they want to be is probably one of the reasons why their self-esteem can be low at times.

I expect most psychologists would agree that the changes that take place in the adolescent's ability to think and reason are one of the most important stages of maturation. At the same time, this stage is often one of the least evident. After all, outgrowing your clothes in a matter of months, having your voice break, or developing breasts are changes that are obvious and will inevitably elicit the "My, how fast you're growing up" comment from relatives. Intellectually, adolescents are also leaving childhood rapidly, although this departure takes place with little public awareness or fanfare.

THE STORM AND STRESS THEORY

"Moody" and "unpredictable" are adjectives parents often use when referring to their teenagers. They can be excited and happy one moment and in deep despair or just plain miserable the next. Stanley Hall coined the term "storm and stress" to describe these swings of emotion. His theory was that, because of all the changes taking place, adolescence was inevitably a period of much tension, conflict, and turbulence. Even though this notion became popular among psychologists, it hasn't been supported by the research.

Contrary to Hall's prediction, it seems only a minority of teenagers go through a lengthy period of instability. Failure to find general support for the notion of "storm and stress" does not, however, mean that the adolescent years are supposed to be smooth or that you're alone if you have secretly sent off for brochures on boarding schools in the Arctic Circle. There's no doubt that most adolescents do experience a faster and more dramatic rate of change in their moods than adults.

An interesting way of studying these mood fluctuations was developed by two social scientists, Mihaly Czikszentmihalyi and Reed Larson. They provided teenagers with pagers and proceeded to contact them at random to find out what they were doing and how they were feeling. (I wish I'd thought of this first. I'd have paged them at 10 o'clock on a Friday night and 7 on Sunday morning; the first time out of curiosity and the second for revenge.) It was found that some, but by no means all, of the teenagers experienced dramatic fluctuations in mood over relatively brief periods of time. An important finding was that these fluctuations didn't seem to indicate psychological difficulties. The teenagers who had the greatest mood swings seemed to be as much in control of their lives and appeared equally as well adjusted as their more even-tempered counterparts. Doubtlessly they were less fun to live with, but it seems it was their parents' sanity, rather than their own, that was being threatened.

You're also far from alone if you feel arguing has become your teenager's favorite pastime. We actually have detailed statistics on this topic. On average, high school students become involved in 0.35 arguments a day. The average length of the argument is 11 minutes. (I didn't keep records, but I think our first two children—now grown up—overindulged themselves and used up their quotas by the age of 15.) The arguments are most frequently in the home and involve both siblings and parents. When they occur between teenagers and parents, the majority involve mothers and daughters.

The conflicts between parents and teenagers certainly add nothing to the quality of life. My brother and I spent most of our adolescent years making sure that any love between us was well and truly masked by running warfare. When we weren't arguing with each other, we were often disputing one of the house rules. How clearly I recall my mother looking at us and stating with conviction, "I should have had goldfish instead."

Just as mood fluctuations aren't usually a sign of any serious psychological problem, conflict between parents and teenagers doesn't necessarily seem to be unhealthy. Some psychologists have even argued that, in moderation, conflict can be beneficial as a means of helping teenagers separate from their parents. This could, of course, be rampant rationalization, but I take some comfort in believing that all of the grief may have been worth it.

RATES OF CHANGE: THEIRS AND OURS

For the adolescent, so much changes within a brief period of time. In an effort to remain sensitive to how rapidly my teenagers were developing I used to compare their pace of life with my own. In one short year my son began driving and had his first girlfriend, job, and hangover. The highlights of my year were turning 40, winning a ham in a raffle, and becoming vice-president of the PTA. As far as I was concerned, I had a good year, but there was simply no contest when it came to deciding whose life was more exciting and memorable.

The different rates of change between parents and teenagers can make life stressful at times. After all, it's much easier to live with people when they change at a similar rate. When I think of my marriage, for example, I acknowledge that both Kathy and I are, in many ways, not the people we were when we embarked on life's journey together. My version is that she's become more mellow and reasonable, while I've come even closer to the pinnacle of perfection. Her version might be quite different, but this is my book. Although the changes haven't occurred in the absence of conflict (believe me, they haven't), we've had the time to gradually accommodate to one another. By comparison, the rate of change in our children during their adolescence was so much faster and seemed much harder to accept.

Keeping pace with our teenagers' development isn't easy. Theirs is a stage of dramatic physical and psychological change, and the period from the onset of adolescence to adulthood spans only a few years. Because of our different rates of change, we may see them as inconsistent, impulsive, and unstable; in their eyes we may be staid, boring, and much too predictable.

CHAPTER 4

PARENTING STYLES

WHAT IS A PARENTING STYLE?

I doubt that many of us think of ourselves as having adopted a particular style of parenting. We certainly have values and attitudes that are important to us, and we incorporate these into our dealings with our children. We have opinions about how much control they should be given and probably have our own way of establishing rules and consequences. Some of our rules come from books and some from remembering how we were raised as children. We borrow ideas from parents we know, and we use our creativity to help develop an approach to family life that seems to fit.

Given that few of us have a set recipe to follow, or would be able to follow one if we did, each family can, in many respects, be seen as unique. By comparison, psychologists usually refer to only a small number of parenting styles. I've limited myself to four; three are discussed in this chapter, while the next chapter is devoted to the fourth. Limiting the discussion to only four styles may seem at odds with the view that families are unique. Trying to pigeonhole every family into one of the categories or styles would, in fact, be an impossible task and probably not a sensible one to undertake in the first place. I can't look at my own family, for example, and conclude we belong to any one category.

So why talk about parenting styles? It's a useful way of focusing on some of the more critical aspects of the approaches or philosophies we bring to family life. Like many parents, I believe, for example, that issues regarding who should be in control, the extent to which family rules are negotiated, and how communication is developed are very important and need to be addressed frequently throughout the course of children's development. Describing different styles provides a way of highlighting the various ways these issues can be addressed. Each style consists of a set of attitudes and values that will influence the way parents see both their own roles and responsibilities and those of their children. These attitudes and values will also have a direct influence on how we actually behave toward our children.

Perhaps the more convincing argument for considering parenting styles, however, is that they have a significant effect on children's development. A recent study in Canada tracked 23,000 children. The researchers were particularly interested in the impact of family structure—for example, the comparison of single-parent and two-parent families. To their surprise, they found that parenting style had a stronger effect on the quality of children's lives than either family structure or income. As the chief statistician for the project commented in the media, "Parenting style matters and it matters one heck of a lot."

AUTHORITARIAN STYLE

The authoritarian style of parenting is the one usually held up as an example of what not to do. Authoritarian parents give orders and expect immediate obedience. They set very rigid rules, and only they have the right to change them. Their children are supposed to passively follow directions and never question the parents' right to govern. Should the children dare to question their parents' absolute authority, they're immediately assumed to be rebellious and disrespectful and in urgent need of punishment. Negotiation simply isn't a term in the authoritarian parent's vocabulary.

I've met many employers who would readily match the above description, as would numerous politicians around the world. Actually, speaking as a parent, the authoritarian style has a certain appeal. It would definitely make life a lot easier. It's a statement of fact that if everyone in my family would do exactly as I want them to do, things would run much more smoothly. My wife also agrees that blind obedience to the head of the household is a very attractive proposition. Our hope is that extending the negotiations for yet another decade will lead to a decision as to who should occupy this exalted position.

At this point I suppose I should be slamming the authoritarian style of parenting, listing all the problems it causes. I'll get to that later, but for now I want to dwell on the merits of being a benign dictator. I can certainly agree that dictators and teenagers rarely enjoy good relationships and that authoritarian approaches to child-rearing need to be modified greatly during the adolescent years. But this raises the question of why the authoritarian approach might have developed in the first place. I work on the assumption that most of us are semi-rational and that, unless proven otherwise, our behavior reflects at least a smattering of good sense.

If you look at the first few years of life, how much room is there for discussion and flexibility? I've never "negotiated" a diaper change or viewed burping the baby as optional. Seeing a toddler about to determine whether or not a spoon can be inserted into an electrical outlet has never prompted me to explore choices with the child or evoke the principle of "natural consequences." Having young children in bed by a certain time isn't, in my opinion, a flexible matter. Rather, it's one of the safeguards I take to preserve what is left of my sanity. If my child wants to tell me why she dislikes school, I'll probably listen sympathetically. But if she tells me she wants to quit at the end of grade three and embark on a career as a bird scarer, I'll break the news to her that she was born 200 years too late, encourage her to revise her career goals, and ensure that she's on the school bus the next day.

We don't give young children many choices. When they become verbal we may take the time to explain why we want them to do something, but make no mistake, they're going to do it no matter what. Traces of authoritarianism aren't hard to detect. I recall a visit from a friend and her three-year-old, Jenna. Not finding our company that enthralling, Jenna took her colored markers and set off to create her own entertainment. Her mother sensed that, even though our kitchen walls were dreary, we might not appreciate the mural Jenna seemed to have in mind. Reasoning, re-direction, and warning looks slowed her down for a moment, but Jenna was on a mission. Then came the telltale sign that a parent is about to slip into the authoritarian mode—counting. "I'm counting to three—one, two . . ." In keeping with my rebellious youth, I secretly wanted to yell, "Go for three, Jenna!" but I exercised restraint and, as expected, she capitulated after two. I suspect that by the time she reached kindergarten Jenna joined the generation of children whose experiences with the authoritarian side of parenting have engendered a deep fear of the number three. I have an image of her being asked to count to 10 and reciting, "one, two, four, five . . ."

I used to believe that I typically gave our children choices when they were younger. What convinced me of my error was taking the time to observe myself in action with my children and make a note of examples of my "negotiating." When our son was four, one of his favorite forms of entertainment was to kick his baby sister under the table during mealtimes. I think this was Aaron's first major experience with the lawful nature of the universe. He learned quickly that even a gentle tap guaranteed a loud screech from Kiera. Of course, Aaron insisted he never kicked his sister. He tried to convince us these incidents were accidents caused by the random motor activity in his legs. The observation that these "accidents" were always accompanied by a broad grin on his face left no doubt, however, as to the truth of the situation.

All of us value peace at the dinner table, so I decided to enter into negotiations with Aaron. "You have a choice. You can either stop kicking your sister or you can sit on the stairs. You will sit on the stairs until bath time and you won't get any dessert. What would you like to do?" Now I suppose that could be seen as a choice. After all, I didn't tell him he had to stop kicking Kiera. But this reasoning is suspect. An example in the adult world would be an employer saying, "Marshall, you have a choice. You can either undertake this assignment or you can empty your desk and collect your vacation pay on the way out."

Over the course of several weeks the list of so-called choices grew longer. Aaron was told he could choose between not spraying his sister with the garden hose and sitting on the stairs, putting his toys away and sitting on the stairs, apologizing to his sister for calling her a "do-do head" and sitting on the stairs, and not using his sister as a toy submarine when they were together in the bath and sitting on the stairs. (You may have noticed certain patterns. First of all, Aaron certainly seemed to have opinions about his sister that we didn't share. Also, we lacked imagination when it came to the second part of each choice. How people who live in bungalows or apartments cope with children is beyond my comprehension.)

Maybe we don't give children as many choices as we believe we do. And probably we shouldn't. During adolescence there will also be situations in which choices aren't given. Rules such as no drinking, complying with a curfew, and not swearing may not be negotiable. There may be some room for the teenager to have input into the nature of the rule, but the parents will insist that one is established. An important part of being a parent is having the confidence and assertiveness to provide clear expectations and standards for behavior and to insist that our children follow the rules. I see these features of the authoritarian style as assets. Of course, if a parent knows only how to be authoritarian and arbitrary, they can expect to have problems, particularly as their children enter adolescence.

I'll discuss the disadvantages of being overly authoritarian in a moment; for now I simply want to make the point that parents start the process of child-rearing by having extensive and arbitrary control over their offspring. Hopefully, we'll exercise this power wisely, but I see no reason why it should ever be given up completely.

As one of the modern leaders in family therapy, Salvador Minuchin, has stated, "The challenge of adolescence is to balance the right of the parents to feel they are in charge with the need of the adolescent to gain independence."

Now to the problems. If the authoritarian style is adhered to rigidly, it's very difficult for children to develop the skills and self-confidence needed to cope with the adult world. They don't learn to negotiate. Asserting their opinions in a reasonable way, while at the same time listening carefully to others' viewpoints, isn't a process with which they're familiar. Rather, they're brought up believing that much of what goes on between people is a battle in which there will be a winner and a loser; someone has to prevail and domi-nate. Ideas aren't debated and opinions aren't sought from others. Children raised in this way are likely to see the world in black and white, and this rigidity breeds intolerance; compromise isn't a word in their vocabulary.

We know from research that children in authoritarian families have little self-reliance. It's hardly surprising they have difficulty thinking for themselves when they've learned from experience their opinions don't count for much and have little, if any, influence on what happens. We also know they're likely to be distrustful; they tend to view relationships as a struggle for power and control. They may be rebellious; on the other hand, they may be passive and submissive. Either way, they're more likely to be unhappy people who don't view themselves as competent and worthwhile.

Before panic sets in, you haven't necessarily condemned your child to psychological purgatory if, in the last week, you've responded to her "why should I?" with "because I said so." What the research has told us, however, is that if we don't encourage our children to voice their opinions and become part of the decision-making process in the family, they'll suffer as a consequence. Sometimes parents hope that emphasizing obedience will encourage their children to be respectful. It might, but there's a real risk it will breed resentment and a lack of respect—both for themselves and others.

MANAGEMENT BY GUILT

Management by guilt (MBG) is a form of psychological warfare. For the child it's like having to live with Dear Abby and Miss Manners at the same time. The hallmark of MBG is a facade of freedom. The children are conned into believing they can make up their own minds about all sorts of things. The parents will state their own preferences but won't forbid their children from going against their wishes. Consequently, no obvious punishment is imposed if the children ignore the suggestions (not rules).

But there's a catch. Going against the wishes of MBG parents carries a huge price. Children will be made aware (repeatedly) of how much damage they're doing to themselves and others. Good MBG parents are excellent nonverbal communicators. With no more than a brief glance and a faint sigh they can communicate how hurt and disappointed they are. They don't have to be asked what they think when they read a report card. The way they hand it back expresses all too well how they've worked so hard all these years just to make sure their children can have a good education and how they've let them down miserably by failing to become star pupils.

Seasoned MBG parents rarely, if ever, get angry at their offspring directly. If children do get a lecture it's most likely to be an updated report on how the lifespan of loved ones is being shortened by their behavior. They're told, for example, that they're at liberty to go to the family reunion wearing their nose ring but are warned that granddad's pacemaker may not withstand the strain.

Another hallmark of the MBG style is over-generalization. The parents look at one particular event or behavior and automatically make sweeping generalizations. The brightly colored hairdo serves as a worthy illustration. Now, I can appreciate why parents lack enthusiasm about being seen in public with a son or daughter who resembles a beacon. The parents' concerns, however, go way beyond the hairstyle's lack of esthetic appeal. Rather, they present it as irrefutable proof their offspring has begun the slow slide into the abyss of sin and degradation. They're truly worried that all their attempts to instill moral values in their child have been fruitless and they have, therefore, failed miserably. I don't doubt their concern is genuine; they're caring people who are beginning to believe their efforts to be good parents have come to nothing. But more often than not I look at the young person in question and get the impression of just a regular kid with a funny-looking head.

I don't want to imply that families come to see me because they're concerned only about hairstyles. Typically, there are several areas of conflict that are upsetting everybody. But what sometimes emerges is that these problems aren't that severe or unusual. The tendency to over-generalize, however, can transform a reason for concern into a cause for alarm and panic. Strange hairdos, listening to heavy metal music, and multiple earrings become signs of being in league with satanic forces. A single hickie is viewed much like a positive pregnancy test, and a beer cap found in the wastebasket justifies the diagnosis of alcoholism.

MBG parents also share some of the rigidity of the authoritarian style. But there's a difference. An authoritarian parent tends to say, "This is the only way because I say so." The MBG parent's viewpoint is, "This is the only way because this is what society expects." The goal is to ensure the child conforms to the standards and expectations of others who are held in high esteem, such as neighbors, teachers, friends, or relatives. The child is taught to be very sensitive to their opinions: "What will so-and-so think if you do this?" is a question they hear frequently in one form or another.

A feature of this style is "parenting by comparison." Other young people are presented as paragons of virtue and shining examples to follow. The skilled MBG parent has a readily available repertoire of "why can't you be like . . . ?" questions and an extensive list of names that can be inserted in the blank. These names are used carefully and selectively. When the issue is schoolwork, the parents insert the names of students who have a permanent place on the honor roll. When discussing chores, they can cite examples of young people they know who willingly rise at six on weekends to vacuum the house, do the laundry, and mow the lawn. Somehow it's usually the case that those held up as models and standards are among the leading contenders for the "most disliked person" award; parents rarely compare their offspring to people they'd see as "cool."

I hope no one working with families would ever maintain that parents shouldn't set standards for their children. Problems tend to arise, however, when MBG is used frequently. As can happen in authoritarian families, the young person doesn't readily develop self-reliance. Excessive concern regarding other people's opinions can breed a self-consciousness and anxiety that inhibits psychological and social growth. Adolescents can spend too much time worrying about how they look to the rest of the world and become preoccupied with trying to secure approval from others. If they don't rebel they may become excellent conformers, but it's unlikely they'll have a strong sense of their own identity or values.

I've found it very interesting and helpful to talk to adults who have been raised in MBG families. Twenty or thirty years can have passed, but they continue to have vivid memories of how they often felt they'd failed to live up to the standards their parents set for them. What has made a particular impression on me is the extent to which they seem to be stuck in the past. It's as if they're still trying to prove something to their parents. Lodged firmly inside them is the belief that they're just not quite good enough; it's like a family version of original sin.

Several years ago I helped run a number of assertiveness training groups—the type of group where you learn how to return defective merchandise to department stores and stop people pushing in front of you in movie lineups without resorting to primitive forms of violence. Thinking back to these groups, I recall the frequent discussions about why self-assertion was difficult. Often the influence of upbringing was raised. Many of the participants described having been brought up in what I'd characterize as MBG families. Stating their own views and asserting their wishes had always been a difficult task unless they could feel certain that other people would give their approval. Somehow they hadn't learned to trust their own judgment or see their opinions as being as valuable as the next person's.

The balance between conformity and independence is always delicate. People who assert their own wishes and viewpoints and show no concern for those of others are likely to become terminally obnoxious. The risk for young people in MBG families, however, is that they'll develop a nagging feeling of self-doubt and inadequacy that can remain with them long into their adult lives.

PERMISSIVE STYLE

This is the laissez-faire style. Accept; don't challenge or criticize. Recognize that everyone is an individual with rights equal to your own. Don't impose your will on your children: you'll crush their spirit. After all, do you want to raise and nurture a human being or create a robot? (By the time my first child became an adolescent, a robot sounded pretty good to me, but the only wisdom I've ever aspired to has been in hindsight.)

I have a particular interest in the permissive style, as it had a strong influence on my early years as a parent. I'd been very much part of the beat/hippy/flower-child generation of the sixties. In many ways this subculture was therapeutic for me as it allowed me to channel my rebellious nature without being incarcerated. One of my strongly held beliefs at that time was that we should run countries through consensus rather than giving individuals the power to control us through governments. So when I became a parent I was bound and determined not to treat my children in an authoritarian manner. I was still a rebel at heart with a dislike of traditional hierarchies. The idea of a family headed by parents was as distasteful to me as a country headed by an elite few. After a few years I became a single parent and was able to allow my philosophy full expression. Joanne and Tim began to call me by my first name, and I placed them in an alternative free school system. I didn't impose limits or set rules. These were discussed with the goal of reaching consensus. My voice was only one of three.

I still have a photograph of Tim when he was four. My sister-in-law took it out of disbelief and in the knowledge that she could use it to cause me endless embarrassment in the future. It shows a boy who could be a candidate for a starring role in a Dickens movie. Most striking is his hair; Tim had no use for a comb and hairdressers weren't his friends. I had no wish to force the issue, so his hair is matted to the point where it looks like a failed attempt at braiding. As for his outfit, he'd chosen to wear his maple-leaf swim shorts over his jeans, and I wasn't about to stifle his creativity. My wife-to-be stared in disbelief as he prepared to leave for nursery school. She'd intended to take him that day; I couldn't understand why she quietly but emphatically refused to leave the house with him.

I was a firm believer in self-expression. If Joanne threw something, I was understanding. "She needs to express her anger," I'd state calmly to myself as I swept up the pieces. If she swore I knew it was because she had to release her feelings; this was much healthier than keeping it all inside and developing ulcers. Meanwhile Kathy (who was beginning to doubt that she was my wife-to-be) shook her head and began totally revising her view of mental-health professionals.

There were times, however, when my calm, permissive approach dissolved. Kathy loves to remind me of the occasion when Tim took the scissors to the couch in a fit of rage—quite proficiently I should add. "Laissez-faire" wouldn't capture the mood that evening; I was apparently as understanding and tolerant as Attila the Hun with a hangover.

The permissive style of parenting lives on, although it has different faces. It no longer tends to be part of a rebellious subculture. In one form it's far more child-focused than it is a reflection of any general attitudes toward society. The parents' intentions are excellent; they value individuality and self-expression as much as I did—and, I hope, still do. They truly understand the enormous potential of children to develop, achieve, and create. To help develop this potential they often spend a great deal of time with their children. If a child seems interested in a particular activity, this is encouraged. The parents facilitate rather than direct. They provide opportunities; they rarely insist. The child's opinions are also given considerable weight. There's much encouragement to express views and feelings, and there's the belief that children's potential includes the ability to make good and rational decisions.

As I write I'm reminded of my continuing belief in certain aspects of this type of permissiveness. I share the view that if we offer appropriate opportunities, our children's interests and potential will usually develop in healthy ways. But this approach to child-rearing can lead to conflict. I tend to find this arises when the child is becoming more involved with groups outside the immediate family—for example, when he begins attending nursery or elementary school. In most educational systems there are clear expectations for conformity. A wide variety of activities is available, but most aren't seen as optional. There are lessons; there are times to do math, and there are other times to write in your journal. There are also prescribed ways of carrying out these activities.

The parents' dilemma is how to balance their belief in the importance of individuality and self-expression with the growing demands that their children conform and learn to fit in with the group. The fear behind this dilemma is that conformity will stunt growth and that the price to be paid for becoming a member of the group will be both loss of self-reliance and suppression of their child's unique potential. As long as the dilemma remains unresolved, the child can find himself becoming more and more in conflict with others.

There's a second form of permissiveness I encounter. This has more to do with the parents' abilities than their attitudes. The permissiveness is by default; it's not an approach chosen by the parents, but is one that develops because the parents are simply unable to exert sufficient control. Sometimes adults who are extremely confident and capable in many areas of their lives find they simply don't know much about discipline. Attempts may be made to impose limits; these often end in the parents' backing down in the face of the child's defiance. If the parent is victorious, this is only after a battle that leaves everyone feeling upset and angry.

The parents may be very loving and sensitive. Their love and sensitivity may, however, be working against them in some ways.

One reason underlying their inability to exert control can be their unwillingness to act in ways that might cause the child to feel denied or disappointed. Children become aware of this "softness" quickly and have no difficulty learning how to melt their parents' hearts.

Whatever the underlying reasons, the parents are faced with the reality that they don't know how to assert their authority. They may complain bitterly about their children's behavior, and often with good cause. But they feel at a loss when addressing such questions as how to ensure their child goes to bed before midnight or how to stop his using bad language or watching television for hours on end. A pediatrician in our community refers to some children as needing to be "bitted and bridled." Having a love of horses, I don't find this comparison between children and colts or fillies at all offensive. It also seems an accurate description of what needs to happen when permissiveness has led to the type of severe and recurrent conflict that can take most of the joy out of family life.

The impact of permissiveness on children has been studied for over 30 years. Permissive parents have been defined as those who, although often warm, make few attempts to control their children's behavior. They tend to impose relatively few demands or expectations and allow their children to regulate their own activities. Like the children from authoritarian families, those from permissive environments tend not to be self-reliant. In fact, the permissive style is likely to inhibit self-reliance even more than the authoritarian style. The hope may have been that, by not subjecting children to external controls and expectations, they'll develop their own standards and will become confident in their own abilities. Apparently this isn't so. An overly permissive home environment is likely to leave children without either a clear sense of direction or the ability to trust their own decisions.

When describing children from permissive families, researchers have used the term "delayed socialization pattern." Part of this pattern is the lack of self-reliance I've just discussed. It also involves poor self-control and lack of social competence. There seems to be a risk that giving children too much freedom will encourage them to develop into self-centered people who disregard the feelings and rights of others.

The permissive style also affects the motivation to achieve. Children need to have standards and objectives set for them. Later on they can take over responsibility for establishing their own goals, but they must first have the experience of working toward those provided by others.

I find it interesting that children themselves seem to be dissatisfied with the permissive style. I suspect most adolescents would be happy to tell you about how parents as a breed are too bossy and controlling, and they may believe they'd be much happier if they had free rein to manage their own lives. Research has indicated, however, that those who find themselves in this position are often far from satisfied with their relationships with their parents.

CHAPTER 5

CAN FAMILIES BE DEMOCRATIC?

We owe much of our understanding of parenting styles to Diana Baumrind. She's a psychologist who has studied the nature and impact of different approaches to parenting for over three decades. Her favorite is by far the "authoritative" style, which has been described as a "rational, democratic approach that recognizes and respects the rights of both parents and children." I'll use the term "democratic" to discuss this parenting style. I find that drawing parallels with political democracies can be useful; the term also avoids confusion with the authoritarian style, which is definitely not on Baumrind's recommended list.

SO NOW WE HOLD ELECTIONS?

There's always a danger parents will equate a democratic family with anarchy and loss of control. After all, one of the principles of democracy is "one person, one vote." Under this principle, holding on to a majority would mean you could have only one child. Panic would set in if you gave birth to twins, with polygamy being the only way to restore the balance of power. Rather than adopt such fanciful solutions, I advocate the selective use of democratic principles. In other words, we (the parents) adopt only those principles we think will be useful and ignore those we don't like. Sounds pretty authoritarian, but let's indulge ourselves.

In my early years as a parent I subscribed to the "one person, one vote" principle, which, in effect, meant that everyone in the family had equal power. I'm not sure what finally led me to abandon this notion. Perhaps it was my growing awareness of the vulnerable position I was in as a single parent with two children. If Joanne and Tim could ever have agreed on anything, they'd have taken complete control of the family. Perhaps I also became more accepting of the fact that democratic societies need to have hierarchies; we choose people to have more power than the rest of us. Whatever the reason, one day I had a revelation. It was a thought that had instant appeal as a way of fending off the chaos I sensed developing in the family. I wanted us to remain a family in which power was shared. But, I reasoned, democracies have a prime minister or president. Someone has to occupy that position. Forget elections. I was obviously the most qualified, and my children were promptly relegated to the backbenches. Under our new constitution my term of office was about 20 years. A little long, perhaps, but it's a tough job and someone has to do it.

Having established who the leaders are in the family, the task is to write the other guiding principles of the constitution. It's hard to select just a few of the principles of a democratic society that seem applicable, but here are some that are particularly relevant for families of teenagers.

CONSULTATION AND COMMUNICATION

The first principle is that people have the right to free speech and, in most instances, the right to be consulted when major decisions are made. The government that doesn't listen to its citizens enough may well pay the price at the next election. But since we've abandoned the idea of elections in families, the parents have the responsibility of ensuring they invite opinions and feedback.

Whole books have been written about listening and communicating. I simply want to suggest to parents of adolescents that they take a careful look at the way communication takes place in the family. There are several questions I recommend parents ask of themselves. The first is: do you actively seek and invite your son's or daughter's opinions? Like many parents, I probably don't discuss matters in the family as much as I should. It's tempting to leave well enough alone when there don't seem to be any problems. Unfortunately, "leaving well enough alone" can all too easily become "letting things slide."

Kiera once reminded me of our failure to communicate about issues that were important to her. It was her dish night, which, as always, evoked groans, sighs, and creative forms of procrastination. As I passed through the kitchen she felt a need to inform me yet again that the chores weren't fair. I was about to give her my standard reply in which I explain that part of my job as a parent is to help my children learn how to cope with the injustices in the world and that doing dishes was, therefore, an excellent learning experience for her. But then it occurred to me that I'd written about the value of communication several times; perhaps some of the ideas in my books actually worked.

Having been asked to explain her point of view, Kiera reminded me that her sister didn't have to do dishes at all. She could understand that Alexandra had escaped this chore previously as she was three years younger, but she felt the time had long since come for her sister to take a turn. I was somewhat embarrassed to realize that in spite of my sincere belief in the importance of regular communication, we'd neglected to review chores with the children and ask them for their opinions and feelings. The matter was resolved to Kiera's satisfaction, and we now have one more child who groans, sighs, and procrastinates when dishes are to be done.

I see the parent's job as creating opportunities for ongoing discussion of the kinds of issues that so often create conflict, such as chores, bedtimes, curfews, school work, and restrictions regarding social activities. Sometimes families have a routine, such as always having an open discussion during Sunday supper. For other families this may seem too formal. Whatever system is used, the question remains simple: do you ask for their opinions? You may feel this is unnecessary; parents often complain of being bombarded by their teenagers' opinions. But even if you feel you hear from them too much, bear with me and entertain the notion that you should nonetheless invite them to express their views. We all like it when our viewpoints are sought, even when there's no expectation that others will necessarily agree with us. What's important is feeling our opinions are valuable and worthy of consideration. Teenagers are no different; in fact, I believe adolescents have a particularly strong need to feel that what they have to say matters. They spend so much of their lives listening to others at school and in the home. Asking for—as opposed to just getting—your teenagers' opinions sends a clear message that you respect both them and their views.

The second question is: does communication tend to be primarily in response to a conflict or a crisis? It makes sense, of course, that issues are discussed when something is going wrong. A teenager's repeatedly coming home later than a specified curfew shouldn't be ignored. Such incidents, however, aren't usually the ideal starting points for discussion. So often they seem to lead to arguments in which no one is inclined to listen to the other person. A lot may be said, and it's at these times that parents and teenagers complain of being bombarded by one another's opinions. The probability of any useful discussion, however, is low. After all, an offense has been committed. It's like arguing with a judge about a speeding ticket when you've been clocked at 80 in a 50-limit zone. You can try to make the case that the law should be changed and the judge might even agree with you, but you don't change laws in the courtroom.

While communication will inevitably be conflict-oriented at times, it should also be an integral part of family life. This is like the democratic process of reviewing matters through public hearings and debates in legislative assemblies. Inviting discussion when no one is feeling angry or defensive increases the likelihood that family members can express their differing and sometimes opposing views without hurting one another. Communication of this nature is also a way of trying to ensure our teenagers don't lose sight of the fact that discussions are based on caring and love; conflict has a way of masking these aspects of our relationships with our children. Although the content of communication is obviously important, how it's said also has an impact. We know, for example, that adolescents' perceptions of the extent to which warmth and support are communicated by their parents are related to their adjustment and well-being.

The third question is: do you actually listen when the invitation to talk has been given? One of my toughest jobs as a family counselor is asking parents to be quiet in ways that are neither rude nor put me in danger of being seen as siding with the teenager. I can remember one father and his son, Rob, whom I met with over the course of several months, primarily because of conflicts regarding school work. Although I never asked him, Rob's father must have won countless awards for public speaking and debating. He was intelligent, articulate, and humorous. He expressed his views in a well-organized way and always provided ample justification for his opinions. Rob was also bright and articulate, but he was no match for his dad. Occasionally, his father would pause and ask him, "Well, what do you think?" I doubt if the reply was ever permitted to be longer than 20 seconds. It was usually terminated by the "yes, I see what you mean, but . . ." maneuver. (This is an excellent tactic. It halts the other person in his tracks by making him believe you might actually agree with him. It's followed, however, by a lengthy monologue in which you inform the person in no uncertain terms that you really meant, "No, you're dead wrong.")

As I sat listening to the father I was struck by how right he was. Yes, Rob did have the potential to do better. If he spent less time on the computer he'd have more time to study. He could certainly benefit from a study skills program. He was in danger of unnecessarily limiting his options by not getting higher marks, and his father, who had led a varied, interesting, and largely successful life, was speaking from a position of greater wisdom and experience. But the more Rob had to listen and feel powerless in the face of his father's logic and well-reasoned arguments, the more I knew he was becoming quietly resentful and rebellious. His father had been winning the debates. Rob, however, was learning to fight back with his behavior. He knew as well as I did that his father couldn't make him work. Dad might control the debate, but Rob controlled his report card.

I wish I could now tell you of the brilliant intervention I made, with the result that father and son learned to communicate effectively and Rob went on to become a Rhodes scholar. It wasn't quite like that. I did help Rob talk about how hard it was to negotiate with his father. We developed the analogy of a faceoff in hockey, with dad being in the NHL and Rob in Junior B. Both were accomplished players in their own right, but it wasn't exactly a fair contest. Dad did undertake to try to give Rob equal air time. He agreed he didn't need to use the "yes, I see what you mean, but . . . " maneuver. Father and son also made a deal. Rob agreed to quit rolling his eyes and looking out the window when his father spoke. Dad agreed not to shake his head in immediate disagreement or smile in what he admitted was a somewhat condescending way when Rob expressed views that differed from his own. I doubt if the faceoffs ever did become a fair contest, and I have no idea what happened to Rob's marks, but it seemed their debates became more enjoyable and productive.

One family told me they had regular meetings at the supper table and used the ketchup bottle method of ensuring everyone got to express their views. It's very simple. When the bottle is in front of you, everyone else has to listen. And no grabbing. When you want to speak, "Pass the ketchup please" is the way to go. I've never risked it. We use a squeezable bottle, and I have visions of a free-for-all that could get very messy. But again, the method itself is relatively unimportant. What matters is that the family works out an agreement that all members—both teenagers and parents—have to listen as much as they talk. No one gets to be a star performer.

NEGOTIATION AND POWER

Let's assume the family has worked out a way of communicating that ensures everyone feels they have a voice that's listened to and respected. (Everyone also remains entitled to the occasional temper tantrum or irrational outburst, but these are kept to a minimum.)

The next issue to be addressed is how much weight should be given to each person's viewpoint. I've argued it's the feeling of being listened to that's important rather than whether or not other people agree with you. Yet, if I felt I never had an impact on what happens I'd soon begin to wonder why anybody bothered to ask me what I thought in the first place. In democracies people strive to balance the need for the government to have sufficient power to run the country with the right of each citizen to have input into the decision-making process. We all need to feel we have a measure of real power. As the everyday citizens in the family, teenagers also want real power. Sooner or later they're obviously going to get it, even if they have to wait until they're adults. The matter for parents to decide is how much power they should ask their adolescents to exercise and at what stage they should transfer this power.

It's probably the case that adolescents can assume greater responsibility than we recognize. The period of time between young children's dependence on parents to their independence as young adults goes by very quickly, and it's hard for us to be aware always of how much they've grown. In Chapter Three I discussed the changes that take place in children's reasoning abilities as they enter adolescence. By the time children have passed the age of 12 they're usually able to do mentally what we often try to do for them. Parents may tell them at length about the likely consequences of their actions, but most adolescents are more than capable of this mental exercise. They can also work effectively with the abstract and hypothetical. Parents, particularly those with MBG traits, may encourage their teens to imagine how other people think and feel about certain situations. Adolescents can do this just fine; the term used by developmental psychologists is "perspective taking," a skill that's well in place by the teenage years.

Having the abilities needed to make rational decisions doesn't, of course, guarantee that teenagers will make the right choices. On the other hand, it's not a bad start. Like most skills, decision-making needs to be worked on. Sooner or later young people have to start practicing if they're to become proficient.

I favor a gradual and planned transfer of power. I emphasize the word "planned," as the idea is to avoid the development of conflicts in which teenagers are trying to win power while parents are staunchly defending their right to keep it. Often the hard part is deciding what areas of power can be transferred in this way. I suggest thinking in terms of three categories. The first category is "that's the way it is." It should be small and refer only to those situations in which you feel you'll always have to insist on using the authoritarian style. Examples might be drug use, smoking in the house, attending school. In these areas the parents exercise their right to set limits that aren't negotiable and trust their adolescents will realize this rigidity is a sign of caring.

The second category consists of the "let's work it out together" group of issues. This is the largest of the categories and requires that both parents and adolescents learn how to negotiate. First of all, it has to be decided what issues are particularly important to put on the table. Some examples come from a study in which teenagers were asked to identify the major areas of conflict with their parents. High on the list was the amount of time they were expected to be home, including always having to come home straight after school, having to eat supper with the family every evening, and always doing homework in their rooms. These issues are good candidates for the "let's work it out together" category. Maybe some free time between the structure of the school day and the routine of family life isn't so bad, and I doubt the wisdom of insisting that adolescents always eat supper with the family. Knowing that your son is alone in his room in the physical proximity of his books is absolutely no guarantee that any work is being done. I remember one girl I was seeing individually who, at 15, had decided to take a short mental "vacation" during the school year. As a result her marks fell precipitously. Her parents were understandably most upset and in no time at all she realized she had used up all her vacation time for many years to come. One new rule was that she had to spend two and a half hours studying in her room every night. It was fascinating to listen to her describe the list of interesting things she could do in her room. Unfortunately, very few of the items on the list were even remotely connected to achieving at school.

Allowing negotiation of the rules about how much time teenagers spend at home often seems to be difficult for families. Perhaps one reason is we find it hard to accept that, in some ways, the closeness and togetherness we enjoyed with our children when they were young can't continue—at least, not in the same form. What made me decide this issue had to be negotiated was the realization that, if I had to make strict rules to ensure togetherness, perhaps I was missing the point. It's like trying to make people have fun together or like one another.

Other issues parents might consider for inclusion in the second category are chores and other responsibilities in the home, use of the family car, attending church, curfews, choice of friends, attendance at family gatherings, participation in family holidays, and choice of recreational activities. Please note that I'm doing no more than suggesting items for consideration. For instance, the religious beliefs and affiliations of some parents may not permit attendance at church to be negotiable. All I'm recommending is that parents take the time to think about the many decisions they've typically made for their children and work on the assumption that most should be negotiable by the teenage years.

So what does negotiation actually involve? People who are bargaining in good faith want consensus: they want to be able to find a solution that's acceptable to all parties. To achieve this they work hard to avoid conflict. If you invite your teenager's opinions regarding curfews, she needs to understand you may have a different view and she'll have to listen to you as much as you'll listen to her. As long as she discusses this matter with you, negotiation will continue. However, should she opt to engage in heavy eye-rolling, deep sighing, or verbal protests that exceed 70 decibels, the negotiations are over until she can treat you with the same respect you're willing to afford her.

Another critical part of negotiation is to be specific and concrete. Sometimes it's hard to stop negotiations from developing into discussions and then arguments about general principles. Attendance at family gatherings is an issue that can illustrate this point. If, after 30 years or so as part of your own family, you're still getting together regularly, it says something about the strength of kinship. Your relatives may drive you to the brink of despair and insanity at times, but somehow they do offer a certain sense of security and continuity. Knowing that you probably drive them to the same brink also helps reaffirm your faith that the world can be just and fair. Teenagers, however, may not see it this way. For some there may be an incentive, such as an interesting or attractive cousin. For others, watching the grass grow might be a more enticing proposition. If your teenager is one of the many who offer resistance to attending family functions, I give you the following challenge: taking into consideration all you know about your son's interests and preferences, try to come up with a more boring activity than the family get-togethers.

Be specific about your expectations. Does he have to attend all, some, or none of the gatherings? Assuming that the matter is negotiable, the answer has to be either "some" or "none." If the answer is "some," which ones do you want him to attend— every second or third, or just the ones on special occasions such as Christmas or Easter? As long as the negotiation focuses on specific issues like these, there's plenty of room for discussion and compromise. The danger is that the parties will start arguing about principles and generalities. Parents may feel hurt and upset that their adolescents don't seem to place as much value on family as they do. This can initiate classic MBG lectures about how much Aunt Gladys will be hurt if he doesn't attend and how grateful he ought to feel for all his grandparents have done for him. This will be countered by reminding you that all Aunt Gladys does is pinch his cheeks, ruffle his hair, and tell him to run along and play. And, while loving his grandparents dearly, Granddad insists on calling him Jimmy instead of Jim, and Grandma never fails to bring out the family album to show him how much he looks like his dad when he was a boy. So the argument progresses with your espousing the virtues and importance of family involvement, while he tries to get you to see how reunions offer a whole new dimension and meaning to the word "tedium." This type of conflict is never resolved. No one agrees and no solution is reached. The conflict surfaces time and time again. The opposing positions rarely change. Everyone knows what the other is going to say, and no one is inclined to change or modify his or her standpoint.

All the issues that tend to lead to conflict can and probably should be reduced to specific questions. It's easier and more effective to discuss the time adolescents have to be home on school nights than to debate the value of an education or the relative importance of friends versus school. It's also likely to be more productive to discuss which specific jobs around the house will be a teenager's responsibility than to embark on the "you're part of the family too—don't you think you should contribute?" line of reasoning. I admit, every once in a while I don't fight my urge to deliver such speeches, but I know these momentary lapses won't help the negotiations and sooner or later I must get back to trying to work out a specific plan and agreement.

Sometimes parents are concerned that making an item negotiable will invite conflict no matter how the issue is discussed. The expectation is that their own and their adolescent's opinions will be so far apart that compromise will be impossible and they should, therefore, hold on to the responsibility for making the decision. I like to think of the development in organizational theory that has taken place recently. The previous models for business and similar organizations have been mainly hierarchical; for example, there's a president and a board of directors at the top, with power being exercised downward through senior, middle, and junior levels of management. There has been a growing interest, however, in abandoning this hierarchy and establishing a web-like structure. In this structure there's a center of power, but decision-making is a responsibility that spreads out to the other parts of the web. The emphasis is on consultation and reaching consensus, and it seems that organizations using this approach can be very effective.

From a more personal perspective, I've had the opportunity to be part of several committees and clinical teams over the years. Those headed by an autocrat who believes he or she has to make the major decisions to ensure that things get done only revive the rebellious side of my nature and make me want to argue, even if I might secretly agree. When the leader asserts authority only if absolutely necessary, I find myself enjoying being part of a group that, more often than not, willingly shares ideas and quickly moves toward finding a middle ground when opposing views are involved. My experiences with families have been similar. I've seen parents and teenagers who have remarkable capacity to fight with one another show equal capacity to reach a joint decision regarding rules and limits. Often I do no more than suggest how to proceed with negotiations and ask the family for permission to interrupt when it seems the discussion is getting too general and needs to be brought back to specific questions.

I believe the single most important step toward successful negotiating is relaxing the hierarchy and establishing a climate in which everyone's opinion has weight. I've seen teenagers who behave in infuriating, aggressive, and immature ways in an effort to wrestle power and control from their parents show surprising ability to act responsibly when invited to share the power and control. I'm not maintaining that negotiation solves all conflicts; what can often be the case, however, is that a genuine transfer of power can strengthen rather than weaken the family unit. It can also help prepare teenagers for independence by providing them with the opportunity to develop their ability to make significant decisions and reach compromises.

The third category consists of areas in which you're willing to transfer all power. When considering items for the "it's up to you" category, it's tempting to relinquish responsibility for only those decisions that everyone knows are trivial. Being allowed to choose whether or not you'll eat salad with supper or having the right to decide if you'll wear your sneakers or boots may increase your teenager's range of responsibilities, but they're hardly giant steps toward emancipation.

I like to start from the position that almost all items in the "let's work it out together" category should sooner or later be considered for transfer to the "it's up to you" group. Once again, I try to keep in mind that they'll soon be young adults and will likely be making all the major decisions themselves. When I think back to my experiences in the working world and the jobs I've had, I recall always appreciating the opportunity to gradually take on assignments and responsibilities. The "throw you in the deep end" approach to personnel management lacks finesse and invites failure. Perhaps the same reasoning applies to preparing teenagers for adulthood. Gradually moving from the stage of shared control to one in which the teenager has most of the responsibility for her life can reduce the likelihood that she'll go either completely wild or slowly to pieces when she's expected to be independent.

I can remember the joy and relief when we finally decided to let Tim manage his high school career on his own. I have to admit this decision was based partly on frustration; we never seemed able to get him to work as hard as we'd have liked. But the decision also stemmed from the realization that, if he did go on to college or university, we weren't planning to move into residence with him so we could escort him to his classes. We'd also decided that if he chose to work rather than study after high school, we weren't prepared to call every morning to see that he was up and wearing clean clothes.

Of course, age and track record need to be considered carefully. Most parents would never allow their 13-year-old son to stay home alone while they're away on vacation. Similarly, giving total responsibility for deciding when to come in at night would be unlikely to occur until the later teens. Demonstration of the ability to share this responsibility with you effectively in the past would also be required.

I'd like to touch on one area of anxiety that parents can have when it comes to allowing their adolescents to assume the major control over areas of their lives. The concern can be that their role as parents will be totally lost and that their children will be almost like boarders in the house who come, go, and do as they please. My recommendation, however, is that parents begin thinking about what it will be like to have an adult-to-adult rather than adult-to-child relationship with their offspring. With activities outside the home, for example, it can be useful to focus on how adults adapt and modify their behavior to accommodate one another. For instance, my wife usually knows roughly where I am at all times. (This is no longer too difficult. The range of possibilities has become sadly narrower over the years. Excursions tend to be limited to the office, the after-hours medical clinic with the child whose turn it is to have the current family disease, and the supermarket.) I'd like to believe that Kathy wants to know where I am and when I'll be back because she can't bear to be apart from me and that I occupy her thoughts during every waking moment. I have to concede, however, that maybe the reason she'd worry if I were late and unaccounted for would be the panic that would set in at the prospect of having to cope singlehanded with our children, her career, and my debts. So we exchange information about our respective schedules, not because we have to seek permission or approval, but because we care about each other.

Teenagers have equal capacity for empathy. At times they may act as if they're indifferent to other people's feelings, but I don't believe giving adolescents control over their lives encourages insensitivity. To the contrary, increasing their responsibilities when they're ready to do so can encourage them to begin behaving toward you with the degree of consideration you voluntarily show in your relationships with other adults. The essential difference is that you ask, rather than insist. So you'd probably request an approximate itinerary and ask your son to call if he's going to be home later than expected. A smattering of MBG may be necessary, but only to reinforce that you'll worry about him just like you'd worry if your spouse's whereabouts were unknown. A small but well-placed quantity of guilt adds strength to the fabric of any family.

We all know it takes time and consistent effort for adults to be able to live together. I see the final period before teenagers leave home as an opportunity to begin the process of learning to relate to them as adults. This period can become unnecessarily stressful when parents try to maintain the relationship strictly on a parent-child basis.

CRIME AND PUNISHMENT

Democracies allow consultation and negotiation and they give real power to the people. Democratic societies also make laws and impose consequences for those who ignore and break the rules. In families this process is usually referred to as "discipline," another topic that has filled whole books. I'll try to get away with three pages for two reasons. The first is that I can't hope to outdo Barbara Coloroso, whose tapes and books about discipline and "natural consequences" are as helpful as they are entertaining. The second is that I believe many of the critical aspects of discipline have been covered in the previous sections on consultation and negotiation. If parents invite their teenagers to share the responsibility for decision-making, it's an easy matter to ask them to share the task of establishing consequences for not keeping to the rules they've helped make. You might assume that if teenagers are allowed to decide on the punishment for their crimes, the most severe will be having to stay in their rooms between eight and nine on a Sunday morning. I'll endeavor to persuade you otherwise.

I mentioned that, in my permissive days, I enroled my first two children in a free school. This proved to be one of the more sensible decisions I made during this period of my life. The term "free school" is unfortunate. It conjures up images of teachers bound and gagged while the unruly masses fingerpaint on the walls. To the contrary, the school provided an organized and regulated learning environment. The focal point was the daily school meeting in which students were given a large part of the responsibility for establishing rules and consequences. The role of the teachers was interesting. Typically, it wasn't to persuade the children of the need for discipline; rather, it was to help them realize that being hung, drawn, and quartered was perhaps a bit of an overreaction to shoving a fellow student in the schoolyard. There was no messing with these youngsters. They knew they were setting rules that applied as much to themselves as to others. That knowledge didn't stop them from establishing consequences for misbehavior that were guaranteed to have a real and negative impact on the offender.

I recall a session with a mother and her 16-year-old son, Ben. Ben's mother never had to worry about discipline until he turned 14. Before that her son was a quiet and compliant lad who was a pleasure to live with. His mother also tended to be particularly lenient with him because of feeling she needed to compensate for his father's leaving when he was a baby. When Ben stopped being compliant, he stopped in a hurry. By the time I began seeing them, he was on probation, had skipped school repeatedly, and seemed to have "fired" his mother as a parent. He was in danger of being permanently evicted from the home, and the tension in the family was high. What struck me, however, was his ability to negotiate rules and consequences. He wanted to regain his mother's trust and knew that not skipping school was an essential condition. He successfully negotiated with her that if he skipped once, he'd hand over his collection of hockey cards for a month. (Serious business, I might add. He had five 5,000 cards, including one worth 400 dollars.) Three incidents of skipping and he agreed that his mother could sell the collection and he'd be given the money to pay for his room and board in another household. As a sign of good faith, Ben offered to hand over six of his most prized cards that night. While I never learned the outcome of the negotiations, the intentions couldn't be faulted.

While we all want freedom, I'm convinced we have an equally strong desire for structure and controls. I start from the assumption that if I invite my daughter to negotiate curfews, she'll be fair in helping to decide what the consequences will be for breaking the rules. The only point I'd emphasize is to try and ensure the consequences are logical, short-lived, and concrete. If she stays out later than agreed, having to sit at home next Friday evening

helps repay the debt—and perhaps only one Friday night's intern-
ment is sufficient. Losing a right or privilege for months on end
only encourages a sense of hopelessness that fosters resentment and
rebellion rather than self-control. Not being allowed to go out also
meets the criterion of concreteness. What tends to be a source of
unnecessary frustration is to embark on lengthy discussions aimed
at changing opinions, attitudes, or feelings. "Why did you agree
to come in at midnight and not get back until one?" is about as
logical a question as the judge asking "Why were you driving 80 in
the 50 zone?" Unless you're an obstetrician on your way to a multiple delivery, your answer is irrelevant. You sinned and you have
no defense. Your daughter was probably doing no more than living
for the moment and having the type of fun and excitement you can
only envy. At some point she may decide that giving in to impulse
and whim isn't worth the hassle. Until then, be kind to yourself.
Mete out the punishment with a minimum of words, lessen your
chances of a stress-related illness, and trust that the general trend
will be upward.

BENEFITS OF DEMOCRATIC PARENTING

The research is compelling. Baumrind's early work focused on
preschoolers and established that the democratic, or authoritative,
approach had a number of benefits. The children exposed to this
style of parenting tended to be more self-confident; they were more
eager to take on new tasks and seemed to cope with stress better than
children in the comparison groups. Gender stereotypes also seemed
less influential—the girls were more independent and adventurous,
while the boys were more friendly and cooperative.

As data were gathered about the long-term effects of parenting styles, the democratic approach continued to emerge a winner.
It was linked to greater interest in learning, enhanced academic
achievement, and higher levels of social and moral maturity. The
children raised in democratic families tended to be more confident
in their ideas and opinions; they displayed greater self-reliance and
possessed better decision-making skills.

Studies that have looked specifically at the development of moral reasoning highlight the importance of the type of communication emphasized in democratic families. Discipline that incorporates a great deal of discussion and encourages understanding of other people's views and feelings seems to set the stage for more mature moral reasoning later in life. A "sleeper effect" has also been noted. Participation in open discussion and debate about moral issues may not have an immediate influence on children's reasoning. If you wait a while, however, evidence of more mature moral judgment is likely to emerge. By late adolescence it seems these earlier discussions exert an influence. I find solace in the concept of sleeper effects; it can foster confidence that our attempts to plant seeds aren't futile, even though the germination time may be much longer than we'd like.

Susie Lamborn and her colleagues at the University of West Florida have also studied the benefits of democratic parenting in adolescence. They followed many thousands of students over a period of several years and have noted the positive effect of specific characteristics of democratic parenting, such as monitoring, encouragement of achievement, and joint decision-making. One of their larger studies related parenting style to the social development, academic achievement, emotional well-being, and behavioral adjustment of over 4,000 high school students. Those adolescents who had been parented in the democratic style had the best scores on all the measures. Another finding was the importance of balancing parental warmth, acceptance, and involvement, on the one hand, with strictness and supervision on the other. The former qualities have a strong role in the development of self-esteem and well-being, while the latter provide a sense of security from having limits.

The democratic style also encourages children to act responsibly. One example comes from studies of latchkey kids. This term has apparently existed for over two centuries and was coined to refer to children who actually had to lift a latch in order to enter their empty homes. The number of adolescents who take care of themselves before or after school has risen steadily over the past three to four decades. Once children reach their teens they aren't usually referred to as latchkey kids; children often babysit at that age and we assume they're old enough to take care of themselves and others for at least several hours at a time. This topic provides yet another example of how people in the same field can hold widely divergent opinions. Some have argued that the periods of unsupervised time are an invitation to trouble; for others they're an opportunity to become more responsible and independent.

Researchers Nancy Galambos and Jennifer Maggs at the University of Victoria compared sixth-grade children in self-care situations with those who were cared for by an adult. The overall conclusion was that the two groups were very similar; the latchkey children didn't appear to be suffering as a consequence of having to take care of themselves. This was particularly likely to be the case when the parenting style was democratic. It would seem the greater self-reliance and better decision-making skills associated with this parenting style helped them act more responsibly, even when their parents were absent.

One common concern for parents is that negative peer influences will encourage their teens to become involved with drugs or alcohol. Again, parenting style emerges as a relevant factor: democratic parents aren't necessarily replaced by their children's peer group. General parenting characteristics such as warmth and monitoring, together with clear communication of values relating to substance abuse, can reduce the impact of negative peer pressure. Conversely, the more permissive style of parenting has been shown to increase the risk of drug abuse and the onset of a pattern of heavy drinking.

Amy Strage and Tamara Brandt at San Jose University examined the relationship between parenting style and the "mastery-oriented" student. Such a student has confidence in her ability to succeed and is persistent in her efforts to do so. Having a positive perception of authority figures, she's also likely to see instructors as a resource to be consulted when necessary. Over 200 university students were asked to rate aspects of their relationships with their parents. Adjustment and achievement were found to be related to key characteristics of democratic parenting: high expectations combined with a high level of support, and the encouragement of independence and autonomy. The findings also demonstrated that the impact of parenting persisted even when the students were living independently. In fact, the relationship between parenting style and success was equally strong when comparisons were made between students living at home and those who had their own accommodation.

An additional finding may be of interest to those who aren't living in nuclear families. In the previous chapter I referred to the Canadian study in which parenting style was found to be more influential than family structure. While it's true that there's a slightly higher incidence of adjustment difficulties among children in nontraditional families, this is unlikely to be the result of the structure itself; rather, it can indicate the need to pay particularly close attention to parenting style. Single parents who maintain a democratic approach can expect to be as successful as those in two-parent nuclear families. The same applies to blended families, in spite of the fact that stepparents may be coping with a lengthy and sometimes painful period of adjustment.

Taken together, the research provides convincing evidence that democratic parenting has a positive impact in many areas, including the motivation to achieve at school, grades in elementary and high school, social competence, confidence and self-esteem, and career aspirations. It's also associated with a lower incidence of behavior problems and a greater ability to cope with stress. And after all the struggles of raising adolescents, parents receive a bonus; teenagers in democratic families are likely to agree that their parents have been fair and reasonable. To date, it seems they've only admitted this during the course of confidential research studies, but at least it's a start.

ADAPTING AND COMBINING STYLES

Although the democratic style is usually singled out for endorsement by psychologists, I have a soft spot for elements of the other three. Being authoritarian has its merits, guilt is a wonderfully versatile and useful tool, and I owe some of the most exciting and memorable moments of my life to permissiveness. Elements of each style have their place. While we need to know how to discuss and negotiate matters with our adolescents, we also have to maintain the strength and determination to make firm and rigid rules when we believe our opinions and decisions should prevail. And guilt has a definite role in child-rearing. We want our teenagers to have a strong conscience; if they don't possess one by the time they reach adolescence, it's probably too late. I want my children to feel bad when they're insensitive toward others and I want them to be critical of themselves when they aren't striving to use their potential and talents. A permissive style will also be important at times. While I expect them to care about the opinions I and others have of their behavior, I want them to have the ability to stand up for their beliefs in the face of opposition. Consequently, I have to give them the freedom to develop their own standards and values and not rely too heavily on others for approval and acceptance.

Another intuitively obvious fact to consider is that children are very different from one another; what works for one child may not be effective for another. The notion that children's differing temperaments influence the way they are, or need to be parented, has also propelled psychologists yet again into the "nature-nurture" controversy. Those firmly on the nature side of the debate attribute most behavior to genetics. From this perspective, children are born with certain characteristics and traits that will determine their personality. Parents can still have some influence on their development, but investing too much in parenting books is probably futile; they'll unfold as dictated by their genetic blueprints.

The other side of the debate emphasizes the role of the environment. The extremists in this camp maintain that a newborn is a "blank slate"—raw material that parents are free to mold as they see fit. I'm convinced the proponents of this view never had children of their own. If they did, they must have been writing from the rarefied atmosphere of their offices while their spouses were back home trying to figure out why their offspring were so different in spite of being raised in much the same way. The more moderate view, of course, is that both genetics and environment should be seen as significant factors determining development. Nature will set limits; the child's genetic inheritance will define a certain range of possibilities for personality and behavior. How parents nurture the child, however, will determine where she operates within this range. This compromise position hasn't ended the debate; psychologists now argue about the relative contribution of nature and nurture, and I guarantee they'll be going at each other long after your children reach adulthood.

In the meantime—and as long as you remain willing to qualify almost everything you say in this complicated field—it's reasonable to take the position that there are innate differences in temperament that are important to consider when deciding the optimal approach to parenting. Preschoolers, for example, will differ with respect to how emotionally reactive they are; they'll also vary along a number of other dimensions such as activity level, adaptability, attention span, and moodiness. A certain winning combination of traits gives you an "easy" child; this is the model child you show off to family and friends in the hope they haven't read the research and will attribute his delightful manner to your exemplary parenting. If your luck is out, you have the challenge of a "difficult" child. This time you hope that people have read the research and will blame his behavior on your spouse's gene pool. Yet another combination gives you the "slow-to-warm-up" model, while approximately one-third are so mixed up they defy description.

But do these so-called temperaments prove to be stable over time? The answer appears to be a qualified yes. Stability of temperament is most evident at the extremes—for example, the preschooler who is very shy is likely to continue to be so as an adult, whereas the social butterfly in kindergarten will remain the life of the party. Yet it's important not to see such differences in temperament as carved in stone; there's always room for learning and the types of experiences we give our children will have an impact.

To date, there has been little research into the relationship between parenting style and temperament in adolescence. At the same time, these differences will need to be reckoned with at this stage of development. The very active and impulsive teenager who views risk-taking as a hobby may need far more assertive discipline than her more cautious brother. You may find yourself negotiating with her at the bargaining table every day. Eventually you may realize she finds the urge to cross boundaries irresistible, and you'll exercise the executive privilege of arbitrarily evoking closure on the debate. In extreme situations temporary imposition of martial law may be required to ensure she's safe, only to be lifted when you feel you've regained sufficient control. Meanwhile her brother, who rarely needs a boundary and wouldn't think of coming close to one anyway, shows a distinct preference for a narrow and predictable way of life. He needs to be encouraged to take a few risks so he can extend his involvement in activities outside the home. You secretly yearn for the day when he breaks the curfew he hasn't needed, and you can't recall the last time there were any major issues to do with discipline.

A moderate challenge to the idea that consistency is a hallmark of good parenting is also timely. George Holden and Pamela Miller at the University of Texas reviewed almost 100 studies that examined the extent to which parents were consistent in their child-rearing practices. They asked three questions: Do parents use the same approach with all their children? Do they use the same approach at different times? Do they use the same approach in different situations? The results indicated similarities and differences, and they concluded that patterns of child-rearing were both "enduring and different." While there was evidence of consistency, parents adapted their parenting style according to the child they were dealing with and the specific situation. Furthermore, this style was modified over time, presumably because of the child's changing needs and abilities. They went on to argue that the ability to be both consistent and flexible is the basis for sensitive parenting and will help children feel respected as individuals.

When contemplating the many factors that have to be considered when developing and implementing an approach to family life, parents sometimes ask me if they'll ever get the balance right. My usual reply is, "I hope not." First of all, after over 30 years of being a parent I haven't been able to get it right, so why should they? In fact, I now take some comfort in accepting that part of the condition of being a parent is to be permanently imbalanced. What's more, I'm the professional, so if there's a recipe for success I should get it first so I can sell it to them for an exorbitant fee. Finally, I believe parents have to remain open to revising the way they deal with their teenagers. Even if I think I've developed just the right style as a parent, my children refuse not to grow up. Very quickly an approach that seemed to fit for the family will have to be overhauled as the children's needs and abilities change and develop. I see it as healthy to assume there's always something I can be doing a lot better. While research can give rough guidelines and help us avoid some of the pitfalls, the manual for successful parenting doesn't exist. I doubt that it ever will.

CHAPTER 6

SELF-ESTEEM

WHAT IS SELF-ESTEEM?

There has been a great deal of research into how people see them-selves (self-concept) and how positively or negatively they evaluate what they see (self-esteem). What is evident is that our self-concepts are quite complex and become more so as we develop. Not surpris-ingly, young children are relatively unsophisticated in the way they see and describe themselves. They also tend to be concrete and focus on physical characteristics or specific skills. For example, if an eight-year-old is asked to describe himself, a typical response will be: "I am tall and I have red hair. My friends call me Red and I like that. I am on the baseball team and I want to be the pitcher. I love math. My parents work and we live in the country near a lake where I go fishing with my friends."

By the time adolescence is well underway, the young person's self-concept has become more complex. Like most adults, adoles-cents begin evaluating themselves in terms of their beliefs, values, and personality characteristics. Certainly, more superficial charac-teristics, such as appearance, remain relevant and can be particularly sensitive issues in the teenage years. What's added to the self-con-cept, however, is recognition of the importance of other dimensions. Part of a teenager's self-description, for example, might be: "I'm an outgoing person and I try to be understanding with my friends. I worry about the environment and I want to become a biologist so I can help change things. I'm usually fun to be with, but sometimes I just want people to leave me alone. I'm okay at school, but if I don't like the subject or the teacher I slack off." Such statements reflect the young person's capacity for self-awareness and insight. They also demonstrate the emergence of ideals and principles, and we know from research that these characteristics remain fairly stable over time; the values adolescents have tend to remain with them into adulthood.

Given that the self-concept becomes increasingly complex, it's not surprising that psychologists have had difficulty devising adequate measures. It now seems to be accepted that if you want to assess a person's self-esteem, you have to consider many different aspects of self-concept. Researchers have, for example, devised separate measures of how people evaluate their interpersonal skills (social self-esteem). I had a student who devoted her undergraduate thesis to developing a measure specifically of students' perceptions of their academic potential and skill. She demonstrated that academic self-esteem was quite distinct from other forms of self-evaluation. Overall, while there's lack of agreement regarding how many areas of self-concept are important, there seems to be no doubt that the number is high. One questionnaire devised for use with adolescents includes nine areas of self-concept, such as body image, educational attitudes and abilities, peer relationships, family relationships, and emotional characteristics.

In addition to specific areas of self-evaluation, there seems to be a more general aspect to how we see ourselves. This is often referred to as "self-worth." It's a basic belief that we're worthwhile and valued as people. It's the ability to feel good about ourselves even when we aren't being successful at what we're trying to do or are being criticized by others. I'll be focusing on this type of self-esteem, which is probably the most critical for healthy development. The feeling of being acceptable as a person gives young people the confidence to develop relationships and take on new tasks and challenges. As parents we have an important role to play in helping our children see themselves positively. To grow up believing they're worthwhile and likable people, children need to receive positive feedback from those around them, and it's usually the opinions of their parents that carry the greatest weight.

To make matters even more complicated, the way in which young people determine their self-worth changes over the course of adolescence. Jennifer Shapka at the University of British Columbia and Daniel Keating from the University of Michigan found that students in grades 9 and 10 placed greatest emphasis on their physical appearance. The second most important factor was perceived job competence; this probably reflected the fact that many of the students had either obtained their first job or were seeking employment. By grade 11, however, the second most important factor after appearance had become scholastic competence. I could immediately relate to this finding. Like many parents, we've made absolutely sure our children know our opinions on the importance of education. During their early high school years, none of them seemed to respond with gratitude when we shared this insight. Then they reached the second half of their high school careers. While signs of gratitude remained absent, we did hear them talk about the need to study harder. As Shapka and Keating noted, they knew their marks in the higher grades would influence the range of options open to them for postsecondary education and employment.

The same study looked at the gender differences and trends in self-evaluation. Overall, boys and girls were equal with respect to their rating of self-worth. The boys, however, rated themselves higher than the girls in physical appearance and athletic competence. The girls, on the other hand, had a more positive perception of their social acceptance and interpersonal skills than the boys. On a final and encouraging note, there were gains in most areas of self-concept over the high school years. It seemed that much of the insecurity and self-doubt that are often part of the early teenage years had given way to greater feelings of competence. Developing this positive self-esteem helps young people navigate the teenage years. It also reduces the likelihood of both emotional difficulties, such as depression, and behavioral problems, including delinquency and substance abuse.

DEVELOPMENT OF SELF-ESTEEM

We seem to be experts at helping very young children develop a healthy self-image. This is fortunate, as early experiences have a major impact on subsequent development. With no effort at all, parents find cause to shower praise and approval on their infant children. In the first few hours after birth (when most babies look like they've been through the wringer) the new arrival is told how absolutely beautiful and wonderful she is. More accurate adjectives would be "wrinkled" and "squashed," but we all line up for the photo packages available on most maternity floors and prove once and for all that beauty is truly in the eyes of the beholder.

Almost anything an infant can manage to do will be treated as an Olympian achievement. This thought came to mind when I had the pleasure of visiting my niece, Emma, in England and meeting my five-month-old grandniece, Nell. There was no disputing who was the center of attention at the family gathering. The fact that I'd come 4,000 miles and nobody had seen me for several years didn't even put me in the running. We vied for turns to hold her and applauded every little gesture and expression. At one point Nell gurgled at her mother and emitted a few other strange sounds. Emma was delighted and responded with, "Who's the clever girl? You're trying to talk." I was tempted to say, "Actually, she isn't trying to talk. She's just emitting gurgles, grunts, and otherwise strange noises—language development comes later." Remembering that I was counting on Emma for a bed for the night, I bit my tongue.

Much of children's development is due to maturation. Humans are programmed to develop in a certain way and will do so provided they receive adequate physical care and live in a reasonably stimulating environment. You could sell tickets for a baby's first steps if you could predict their occurrence. It's treated as an achievement akin to making the all-star hockey team and is awaited with keen anticipation. I hate to rain on the parade, but it isn't really an achievement. There's not too much learning involved. You don't have to send them to Young Walkers of Canada; just leave them alone and sooner or later they'll get up and walk. Rather than being clever, the baby is simply doing what he's been programmed to do genetically.

And we continue to be liberal with our praise for toddlers. They return from playschool with artwork that defies identification. I'm eternally grateful to the staff who have written my children's names on the painting or drawing as this is usually the only reliable method of determining which way up it should hang. Having been told they've made a picture just for you, what can you say but, "That's wonderful!" Inexperienced parents will follow this with, "What is it?" The more tactful or devious approach is, "Now come and sit down and tell me all about your picture." Having gathered enough information to determine that the seemingly random meanderings of the paintbrush represent a cow as opposed to a house or member of your family, the work is placed with ceremony on the refrigerator door.

If you want a reprieve from the stresses of everyday life, spend an evening watching four-year-olds play soccer. I can remember how loudly we cheered when Alexandra finally ran; weeks later we were ecstatic when she ran in the right direction.

I'm not suggesting we should stop lavishing praise on young children; they need our encouragement and approval to gain confidence in themselves. But somehow things change. The youngster who was so easy to applaud grows up and develops tastes, interests, and habits that are unlikely to evoke curtain calls. We encouraged them to listen to children's songs but threaten to cut off stereo privileges if they persist in playing hard rock. We thought it cute and adorable when they paraded in dress-up clothes but report chest pains at the sight of T-shirts proclaiming anarchy and rebellion. They never put away their clothes, they leave cups and dishes in their room, and cleaning the bathroom sink is beyond their comprehension. They leave more dishes and cups in their room, and you begin to believe that having homework is a figment of your imagination. As yet more dishes and cups find their way upstairs, you give serious consideration to installing a dishwasher in the bedroom, except you'd never be able to get the door open wide enough. The number of issues that lead to frustration and conflict can grow steadily, and a situation can develop in which disapproval and criticism overshadow praise and encouragement.

STRENGTHENING SELF-ESTEEM
BALANCING CRITICISM AND PRAISE

There's an exercise I've used at workshops. I once did it myself and found it quite informative. Each person gets two pieces of paper. You're asked to cast your mind back over the past two weeks and, on the first piece of paper, write down as many examples as possible of comments you've made to your adolescent of a critical nature. You include even those gentle and subtle reminders we give "for their own good." Examples would be, "You wouldn't have that cold if you had worn your woolly toque that Grandma knitted" (perhaps true, but neither would he have any friends); or, "Jeffrey is such a nice boy, why don't you ask him over?" (this usually translates into "the friends you choose are bums or psychopaths"). As a participant, I remember how much we all loved this part of the exercise. It was so therapeutic—pencils were breaking and people called for extra sheets of paper as they vented their frustration. I normally allow a good 10 minutes for this part of the exercise.

I'm sure you've guessed what part two entails. The task is simply to use the second piece of paper to list all those comments made of a positive nature, such as showing approval or giving praise. You don't need 10 minutes for this. When I did the exercise I was already a practicing psychologist and my first reaction was to be somewhat appalled that the vast majority of feedback I gave my teenagers was of a critical nature. After all, I should have known better. But I had a second reaction. My defense mechanisms didn't fail me. I reminded myself that, if my teenagers would act in a more reasonable and civilized manner, I'd happily show more approval and gratitude. Nobody could expect me to give praise where it wasn't due or ignore the faults that were so evident in my offspring.

Unfortunately, the workshop leader was way ahead of me. Before I could begin to present the case for my defense, she announced she was sure many of us would by now be trying to rationalize our critical tendencies. She asked us to go over our list of criticisms and decide how many were really necessary. She gave us some guidelines for deciding what constituted "necessary." If it involved safety, the item should stay on the list—for example, reprimanding your daughter for walking home alone late at night in a poorly lit neighborhood. An item would also be acceptable if it dealt with a new issue, such as a sudden drop in school marks.

It was hard to find items that qualified. I have yet to see a study that links toque-wearing with the common cold or other hazards. As for the suggestion about choice of friends, he already knows exactly what you think of his friends, and there would be no reason to expect that raising this issue yet again would change his behavior.

When I took a good look at my list of criticisms I had to admit the vast majority were unnecessary, repetitious, and ineffectual. How many times did I need to tell Joanne her marks would go up if she spent more time on her homework? It isn't exactly a novel idea. Anyone with two brain cells to rub together can figure that one out. But maybe if I kept reminding her of the relationship between homework and marks she'd start working harder. Forget that. I've already given her the "education is so important—you only get out of school what you put into it" lecture 167 times and how likely is it the breakthrough will come on the 168th? And, Aaron must know the connection between going to school in a wrinkled T-shirt and his practice of throwing all his clothes in a pile on the bedroom floor. In fact, walking on his clothes is the closest I've ever seen him get to ironing them.

Having convinced us that much of the negative feedback we gave our teenagers was both unnecessary and ineffectual, she turned to our second pages—not that there was much to turn to. I think there was consensus among us that we saw our teenagers as basically "good kids"—it just happened that they drove us crazy much of the time. But while we may have thought they were good kids, we rarely seemed to take the opportunity to share this view with them. The task then was to think of examples of ways in which our teenagers had acted in the last week that we liked. I recalled that Joanne had helped with the yardwork and had read a bedtime story to her little brother. Tim had been affectionate toward his baby sister. He'd also been practicing his trumpet diligently for the Remembrance Day service. And while it took effort and concentration, all of us were able to make respectable lists of actions that would warrant positive feedback.

I'm not suggesting we do tremendous damage to our teenagers by the negative feedback we give them, but it certainly doesn't help their self-esteem. To maintain a healthy balance between criticism and praise, our "basically good kids" need to hear that's how we see them.

I'm also not suggesting we abandon opinions and expectations. We're obviously entitled to both. But often we spend a lot of time repeating ourselves in a way that's critical of our teenagers. They'd call this nagging. Not surprisingly, when one group of researchers asked teenagers to list their complaints about their parents, nagging was easily the most frequent.

Lecturing is the more sophisticated form of nagging. I used to deliver many of them, so I find them easy to recognize when I meet with families. One parent usually starts and you're struck by how smoothly and eloquently he's speaking; practice and repetition lead to excellent delivery. The teenager for whom the lecture was written typically slumps in her chair adopting a posture of semi-sleep. While doing so she emits a low groan or soft sigh and rolls her eyes. In some families it's a team effort. The parents take turns, reinforcing one another and presenting a formidable united front. The timing is precise. Each knows exactly when to take over from the other or provide comments to emphasize a point that's just been made.

I always find these situations awkward. The parents clearly want me to be the guest lecturer, perhaps in the hope that a trio of voices will succeed where the duet hasn't. There are two problems with this. First, it's extremely difficult—if not impossible—to work effectively as a family counselor if you take sides. Second, I know I won't be any better at lecturing their offspring than I was at lecturing mine. If I'm lucky, the teenager may listen to me with a facade of respect, but inwardly she'll be slouching, sighing, and rolling her eyes, just as she did for her parents.

I've suggested to some families that they might want to make a tape. I recommend this in all sincerity, as the lecturing can become a source of much frustration. Usually there are a few key lectures that could readily be put onto audio cassettes. At the appropriate moment you simply hand the relevant tape to your son or daughter and tell them to go and listen to it in their room. Whether they play it or not is immaterial—they know exactly what it says. I'm not sure if anyone has actually made such a tape, but perhaps just realizing how unnecessarily repetitious and critical we can allow ourselves to become as parents helps us change.

A far better use of our time and energy would be to review the expectations and rules. Perhaps it's time for the issue we're lecturing on to become the teenager's responsibility with minimal or no parental involvement. Perhaps not. If we decide the issue is one that can't be left just to our teenager's discretion, it may be time to renegotiate the expectations and rules. In yet other situations we may be confident the rules are fair. The job then is to impose consequences in a straightforward, matter-of-fact way. Imposing consequences is usually more than sufficient to register our disapproval. Prolonging the point only encourages unnecessary debate, and teenagers can find themselves defensively trying to justify their actions even when they know they're in the wrong.

SEEING BEYOND THE BEHAVIOR

Many parents are aware of the advice to comment on behavior as opposed to character. "I love you, but your behavior stinks" sums up this approach. But while we may have no difficulty communicating unconditional love for our children, letting them feel we still respect them can become more difficult, especially when there seem to be so many conflicts arising from their behavior. I always try to remind myself that the problematic behaviors I may see in my offspring are not symptomatic of character flaws. Our daughter Kiera made no distinction between chores and slavery. The mere hint we might be about to suggest she do the Saturday morning jobs for which she had already received a hefty advance on her allowance could launch her into her standard tirade. Surely we know her exhaustive survey has established she was the only 13-year-old in the county who was expected to operate a vacuum cleaner. Hadn't we heard of child labor laws and didn't we realize she'd already made plans for the weekend that simply couldn't accommodate menial work that was, by the way, being paid for at below the minimum wage? Though Kiera's aversion to household chores never showed signs of abating, I resisted the temptation to see her as a "lazy" person. If I believed this to be the case, my criticisms would soon have become very personal—to call someone "lazy" or "irresponsible" is to imply they truly lack something that's an important ingredient of self-worth. So I reminded myself that, with very little prompting, she had spent many hours on her science project. If only a fraction of the time and energy she devoted to dancing had been channeled into housework, Kathy and I would never have had to lift a finger at home again. None of these thoughts solved the problem of the Saturday morning battles, but they helped me maintain that critical distinction between behavior and character.

To see beyond the behavior we may need to remind ourselves of the past. Sometimes it's hard not to become overly focused on recent behavior. When families seek counseling it's, of course, because they're going through a period of particular difficulty and stress. Quite often parents are very angry at their children and are exasperated by their attitudes and behaviors. Rarely, however, has the situation at home always been this way. To the contrary, it's far more likely that the period in which there has been conflict is relatively small compared to the total amount of time the parents and children have been together. To help me gain a better understanding of the family, I sometimes spend a session playing "This Is Your Life." I'm a sucker for baby pictures and really don't find other people's family albums boring. So I ask parents to bring these in, and we look at them together. While I'm learning about the family, the parents and teenagers have the opportunity to recall the closeness and positive feelings in their relationship that may have become masked by the recent disputes.

I can remember a 14-year-old girl, Tina, and her mother who were engaged in a major struggle for power and control. At times it seemed they despised or even hated one another, and I was becoming concerned that perhaps their relationship was irreparably damaged. The first time I heard them talk to each other, rather than argue, was when they recalled Tina's trying to pull her front teeth out after she'd learned that, with the good services of the tooth fairy, these were as good as money in the bank. Tina also listened intently to her mother (a new behavior in our sessions) as she talked about what a cute, fun, and lovable baby she'd been. I wanted to know if the closeness had been there, and they needed to be reminded that it had. They agreed that, in a very real sense, they missed one another. The arguments certainly continued, but perhaps reaffirming that they both cared about one another and wanted to become closer again made the conflicts less destructive.

Another aspect of seeing beyond the behavior is to become aware of the important but sometimes hidden ways in which teenagers have developed. When discussing the definition of self-esteem I referred to how attitudes and values become a significant part of adolescents' descriptions of themselves. Sometimes we tend to assume their beliefs and interests are impulsive and likely to be short-lived. In some regards this may be true, but adolescence also sees the emergence of values that often prove to be stable. For example, issues such as individual freedom, social responsibility, and establishing a just and tolerant society become important for many adolescents. Social scientists who have studied development and shifts in values have noted that teenagers are often concerned with matters such as social and economic discrimination, racial prejudice, and pollution.

In fact, they seem to be more involved in such issues than previous generations, and their attitudes reflect a high level of tolerance and flexibility.

It can be hard to be aware of the deeper aspects of your teenager's development when you're confronted with a son who doesn't seem capable of taking responsibility for simple things, such as cleaning the kitchen counter after making a sandwich or putting his clothes in the laundry hamper. Having to deal with these exasperating surface behaviors can create a smokescreen that prevents us from seeing aspects of our children's personalities that we'd probably applaud.

I have a particularly fond memory of a 14-year-old client, Natalie. The family came to see me because of rapid and disturbing changes in her behavior. Natalie had begun wearing nothing but dark clothing, she listened to heavy metal music, she had experimented with alcohol and possibly soft drugs, and she was becoming openly defiant toward her parents. The parents were concerned about her moral development; they'd reached the point where they felt all their efforts to instill healthy values in their daughter had failed. This feeling of failure was becoming very damaging. They were beginning to see Natalie as bad and hopeless; Natalie, in turn, saw her parents as no longer liking or respecting her.

After spending some time talking with Natalie alone I found I had a different view of her. Yes, her behaviors were troubling, but my impression was that her parents had been successful in raising a daughter who had some very fine principles and standards. The one Christmas present she'd requested was a book on world peace, a collection of articles, paintings, songs, and poetry. She allowed me to read some of her poems, which expressed the difficulty she had reconciling her family's upper middle class lifestyle with her growing realization that much of the world's population had to contend with lifelong deprivation and hardship. I was struck by how articulate and insightful she was when discussing her views regarding religion and politics and, in some ways, she made me aware of my own shortcomings. She was expressing a degree of concern about the state of the world that I'd shared passionately as an adolescent. Like many of my generation, however, my social conscience eventually took a back seat to more self-serving goals such as my career.

There was reason to be worried about Natalie's behavior, but there were also reasons to be proud of her. The parents' belief that they'd lost their daughter was generating strong feelings of self-reproach, anger, despair, and pessimism. My goal was to present Natalie to them in a different light—as someone whose behavior certainly needed to be brought under greater control, but whose underlying personality was sound and healthy in many respects. This more positive perception could help them maintain their respect for Natalie despite disapproving of her behavior.

One way in which I became more aware of the depth and quality of my own teenagers' personalities was through reading some of their essays and papers. I was occasionally permitted to read these, as long as I understood my role wasn't that of critic. It was interesting to hear their thoughts and analysis of human behavior arising from books such as *Lord of the Flies* or to become aware they had the ability to wrestle with complex issues such as capital punishment, racial discrimination, and gender equality. I also learned to take the opportunity to ask them more about their views and opinions on topics that were current, such as abortion and the conflicts in the Balkans and the Middle East. Listening to them talk, debate, or argue was stimulating and enjoyable; it also reinforced my respect for them as people. They still rarely cleaned the counter after making a sandwich, and the laundry hamper remained conspicuously empty, but their thinking could be infinitely more mature than their behavior seemed to be at times.

UNQUALIFIED PRAISE

I like to think of praise as a gift. As such it shouldn't be taken back; neither should it be seen as an investment for which we expect some form of return. If you'll allow me to indulge a fantasy for a moment. Imagine that Kiera came downstairs one Saturday morning and announced, "I just love Saturdays. What an opportunity to contribute to the household and, in some small way, repay my parents for everything they do for me. I think I'll skip breakfast and get right to my jobs." There's no doubt that after a prolonged period of speechlessness we'd shower praise on her. The temptation, however, would be to add that we wouldn't have been upset if she'd adopted this attitude a little earlier. In this way, the message becomes mixed: "We think you're a great kid, but . . ." Praise and approval should stand on their own and not be taken away as fast as they're given.

RANDOM ACTS OF KINDNESS

This is, of course, the title of a popular book that gives people's accounts of how touched they were by others' unexpected good deeds. Pigeons react the same way. It's called the "partial reinforcement effect." For over 50 years psychologists have been working on the best way to train pigeons to peck a key; they've been doing it for so long that no one can remember why it's important to gather this information. One discovery has been that giving them a reward every time they peck the key isn't the best way to go. Pigeons are far more impressed when the rewards are spaced out and unpredictable. As far as one can tell, getting a shot of birdseed unexpectedly makes their day, and they'll proceed to peck the key with abandon. It also works for humans. As long as a little bit more is spent on the reward, we too will show more enthusiasm for learning a new behavior when the reinforcement is unpredictable.

A simple example illustrates the power of unexpected reinforcement in everyday life. Flowers on Valentine's Day are usually received with genuine pleasure. Compare this, however, to receiving a bouquet in mid-November with a card that reads: "Just because I love you." Now that's romantic and something to brag about.

Several years ago I consulted at a children's residential treatment center. I recall a staff member describing how she practiced these random acts of kindness. A few examples come to mind. Every once in a while she'd leave a note on a child's pillow with a caring or complimentary message. A child might receive a hug for no particular reason when he least expected it or find a small treat packed in his lunch box with a note such as: "A special treat for a special person."

Younger children seem to receive these random signs of affection and appreciation far more often than teenagers. For no reason whatsoever parents will scoop up their six-year-old and give her a hug—not so easy a task with a 15-year-old with an attitude. But the need is still there, just as it remains throughout the course of all long-term personal relationships. A note, a card in the mail, a favorite dessert, picking them up for lunch, a rose on the dresser, offering to help with a chore just because you know how anxious they are to join their friends, all send a message that, no matter what else may be happening in the relationship, they never lose the status of "special person."

LEARNING TO COPE WITH FAILURE

I admit to being a card-carrying klutz. I like to feel I can be successful in my professional life, but this shows little sign of carrying over into the practical, hands-on aspects of home life. I should have quit before I was too far behind, but I can't shake the belief that men are supposed to know how to fix things—that the presence of testosterone guarantees the ability to use a hammer, repair a leaking faucet, and have instant rapport with a misfiring car engine. Many of our family and friends seem so handy, and this has added to my frustration. Our close family friend Mr. Porter—who must ooze testosterone—has an out-of-body experience every time he hears the sound of a power saw or electric drill. And Mrs. Gabel across the street, who is almost devoid of testosterone, not only assembled a swing set but also polished off a three-burner, every-gadget-imaginable barbecue in an afternoon.

The barbecue irked me the most. I remember the spectacle with shame; it exposed the children to a new vocabulary that would have fast-tracked them to their rooms had it emerged from their mouths. As I sat in the middle of the kitchen surrounded by parts of every size and description, I was faced with the initial challenge of finding the instructions written in English, although I doubt I'd have fared any worse with the Korean version. Over the course of the afternoon I crossed over to the dark side of the force, all traces of social veneer being replaced by raw and primitive emotion. The family rolled their eyes as I launched into one of my tirades that always accompany do-it-yourself projects. They begin with "I don't believe it!" and end with "Never again!"

"Never again!" is a wish yet to be fulfilled. Over the years I've ventured into most of the trades; not a single success comes to mind. My attempts at plumbing have each been followed by an urgent telephone call and a visit from the ever-patient Mr. Porter who has tried to pass along the fundamentals of the blowtorch and snake.

I've also tried to ensure that my children don't follow in my footsteps. Kiera developed an interest in fixing things, so father and daughter went to the local hardware store to purchase her own tool box. I explained the operation of the multi-headed screwdriver and how to use a hammer without inflicting too much personal injury. Having received my accumulated wisdom, she has been left to carry on as best she can.

My experiences as a klutz remind me of the time I spent working at a university counseling service. I met many students who were struggling with the demands of a far more challenging academic environment than they'd encountered at high school. Particularly vulnerable were young men and women who had become accustomed to being "stars." Their many achievements had been earned, and they had every reason to be proud of their awards and accolades. But they hadn't learned how to deal with failure. The first bombed math test was a devastating experience, and my task was to convince them their chances of having a productive and worthwhile life were not completely eliminated. I toyed with the idea of offering a course on how to fail but couldn't decide if a passing mark should be below or above 50.

I've never subscribed to the maxim "you can do anything you put your mind to." As much as effort and determination are admirable qualities, they don't necessarily compensate for lack of talent. We all have gifts, but we also have limitations. Dealing with success is hardly a challenge; it's not hard to praise our children for their accomplishments and make them aware of their strengths and abilities. But they won't always meet their goals. Failure is surely a fact of life. I'm not suggesting we make a point of highlighting one another's deficiencies or refrain from challenging our children. Self-esteem that's based only on being successful, however, is hard to maintain.

By the time children reach their teens they usually have an awareness of their weaknesses as well as their strengths. They may not make the volleyball team and, in spite of studying hard, they may have to face the disappointment of failing a course. Parents have asked how to respond to comments such as, "I guess I'm not very good at volleyball" or "I wish I were as smart as my sister and didn't have to take this course again." My suggestion isn't to attempt to reassure their son or daughter they're just as capable as any other student or be too comforting—the teenage version of "there, there it will be all right" may communicate that the parent thinks it's indeed terrible to have performed poorly in comparison to others.

It can be more helpful to respond in a sensitive but matter-of-fact way. Acknowledging how disappointed their son is can lead to a discussion about whether or not he thinks it would be worthwhile trying out for the team next year. Encouragement to try again may be needed, but so, too, might support for a decision to abandon a particular goal and move on to another. In a similar vein, sympathy for the failed math course is in order and should be forthcoming. But equally important is a practical acknowledgment of the situation: "You're right, she's better at math than you. That may not seem fair, but I'm afraid it means you'll have to work extra hard when you take the course again. Just let us know if we can help in any way." The "so what?" tone is deliberate, and I hasten to add that I'm not recommending a callous indifference to our teenagers' disappointments and failures. I'm suggesting that communicating an acceptance of their limitations helps them apply the same acceptance to themselves. This approach doesn't promote giving up—rather, it makes it easier for them to either try without being devastated by failure or decide to accept that sometimes we all need to set more attainable goals for ourselves.

THE GIFT OF TIME

I can't remember when I first heard the comment that the greatest gift you can give your children is your time. I recall sitting in my office with a 15-year-old boy, John, who was in tears as he recalled his seventh birthday. His father had promised to take him skating— just the two of them. When the day came his father told him they wouldn't be able to go, as he had to visit a friend. The memory of this event continued to have as much impact as it had eight years before because it had been reinforced by several similar incidents throughout his childhood. Sadly, John had come to see himself as someone who ranked low on his father's list of priorities.

There are always songs that have a strong impact on you whenever you hear them. *Cat's in the Cradle* is one that I always listen to intently. It depicts a father who never seemed to have enough time for his son. You aren't given the impression he didn't love his son; it just seemed that other things got in the way. He was busy building a career and this takes a lot of time. There'd always be another day to play ball. But somehow there wasn't. His son grew up and moved away. His father eventually found himself wanting to spend more time with his son. Maybe he was hoping to enjoy a closeness they'd never achieved. But it proved to be too late; his son had his own life in which his father couldn't play a major part.

It seemed the song could have been written about John and his father. The difference was that John was making it clear he wanted things to change. Rather than becoming defensive, his father was open to taking a careful look at their relationship. It surprised him that he was so important to John; it pleased him as well. I quickly became redundant. They knew what the problem was and they were more than capable of fixing it themselves.

Perhaps our time is the greatest gift we offer our children because it's a clear statement regarding how important and worthwhile they are. If you choose to be with someone, you're letting them know they matter to you and you like their company. After all, if I were confronted with people crossing the street whenever they saw me coming, my self-esteem would take a severe battering.

I've often talked with parents who are at a loss to know how to spend time with their teenagers. They no longer want you to read to them or play another game of "fish." You could go to the movies together, but chances are you'd never agree on what to see. You could talk about your day, although this may cause your son or daughter to experience heights of disinterest and boredom that exceed their wildest dreams.

My daughter taught me that being together can be an extremely simple matter. Joanne once remarked that she liked it when I was at home. This surprised me greatly. Joanne's communication at that time consisted primarily of rolling her eyes, banging doors, and heavy sighing (I can still hear those sighs after all these years). It seemed my presence was about as welcome as acne. Then, out of the blue, she remarked that I was away from home a lot and said it in a way that communicated her disapproval. I came to realize that she liked my being around. Sometimes we might sit in the same room; on rare occasions we even talked. At other times she ignored me completely, and I had to work hard to convince myself that my presence in the house mattered to her at all.

Over the course of the years with my children I've also learned there are specific activities we can enjoy sharing. I believe there's usually a common ground between parents and teenagers, although it may be far from being a vast expanse. There's often at least one television program that could be watched together, and junk food (in moderation, of course) can make the event special. Now that I think of it, many of the activities I share with my children center on food and sedentary activity. I know my strengths. For the more adventurous, the North American passion for sports can often provide the link between the generations.

I won't attempt to provide a comprehensive list of what the common ground can be. Once families have set their collective minds to the task, they can be quite creative in thinking of ways to enjoy being together. Quite often the obstacle to their doing this has been the assumption on both sides that neither is interested.

I'm also convinced of the value of spending time with one's children individually. For those of us blessed with more than one teenager at the same time, the difference between our children when they're together and apart can be dramatic. You may have been more fortunate, but as far as I'm concerned, the term "sibling rivalry" could have been invented for my first two. Joanne and Tim had an unbelievable capacity for conflict. If one had offered an innocent "good morning," the other would have immediately responded with a meteorological challenge and off they would go. Squabbling seemed to be their major form of entertainment. (During this period the title of this book came to mind.) Being with them individually was a very different experience. They seemed to be so much older. At weaker moments I even suspected they were rational human beings.

Our lives can be very demanding. Families with two working parents are the norm. We often encourage our children to be involved in outside activities with the result that there's little time left for us to be together. Yet somehow we still need to make sharing time with our children a regular part of family life. They need to know that, whatever other demands are placed on our time, we value their company.

CHAPTER 7

SEXUALITY

ARE WE SMARTER ABOUT SEX? A LOOK AT HISTORY

When people talk about the sexual revolution, they're typically referring to the changes in behavior and attitudes that may or may not have occurred. But what about knowledge? Do young people have a better understanding of sexuality? Do they have the information and facts that are needed whenever we're trying to make rational decisions about important areas of our lives? And how much information should they get? If you tell them too much, will you encourage them to be sexually active? Who should teach them about sex?

Our stage in history is often referred to as the "information age." Sexuality, however, is notably absent from the list of subjects in which most young people are well versed. It continues to be a topic that many find embarrassing and so they don't ask questions or discuss their fears openly. I don't believe this is because sex is so personal a topic it can't help but be somewhat embarrassing. There are cultures in which our taboos about sex simply don't exist and in which the topic is dealt with in a relaxed and open manner. But we had the Victorians. While their era may have brought about many exciting and positive changes in society, they left us with a legacy of myths and anxieties about sexuality that we've yet to bury. This was the generation that advised people to cover table legs for fear of arousing men's passions. Not surprisingly, if table legs were such a hot topic, any more obvious form of sexual arousal or expression had to be a major cause for concern. As an illustration, I want to discuss the most widely practiced sexual behavior and one that received a lot of attention from the Victorians.

Masturbation is the most common form of sexual expression among adolescents. By far the majority of teenage boys and girls masturbate; the estimate for boys often exceeds 90 percent. And it seems the practice has been immensely popular for as long as people have conducted surveys. There's something about the topic, however, that promotes a rapid departure from reason and common sense. Let me introduce you to Dr. Kellogg. His book *Plain Facts About Sexual Life* was published well over a century ago. He devoted a large section of the book to the topic of the "secret vice" and proclaimed: "This sin is one of the most destructive evils ever practiced by fallen man." Having got the attention of his audience, he proceeded to list the symptoms of the secret vice. Telltale signs included stooped posture, eating clay pencils, a taste for spices, and suspicious positions in bed (he left it to our imaginations to determine what these might be). Not eating clay pencils wouldn't be too much of a sacrifice, but having to choose between no cinnamon on your French toast and being seen as a sexual deviant was a bit much.

That's not the half of it. Adolescents suspected of masturbating were forcefully discouraged from continuing the practice. One technique was to place a spiked ring around the penis; an erection under these conditions was far from pleasurable. Another was to attach a device to the penis that activated an alarm if an erection occurred. This brings a new dimension to the image of bells ringing at the height of sexual passion. In light of today's knowledge, these interventions were absurd. Many years ago I published several papers in the area of nocturnal erections. While I hasten to add there was a legitimate reason for this research, I just want to make the point that all normal males spend approximately one-third of sleep with a partial or full erection that has nothing to do with being sexually aroused. So imagine the impact when the local general store got its supply of spikes and alarm systems. By midnight the noise in the neighborhood would have been deafening.

Girls weren't exempt. The bicycle, for example, became popular in Kellogg's time. This wasn't the innocent invention you might have assumed. Bicycles require pedaling and involve sitting on saddles. A Dr. Libby Hamilton-Muncie counseled parents regarding the implications of bicycle riding for their daughters. She suggested mothers have their daughters ride their bicycles naked. The purpose was to prevent the action of pedaling bringing the genital area and the saddle into a meaningful relationship. Again, I'm the victim of an overactive imagination. Where did these inspections take place? Hardly in the front parlor. On Christmas morning was there really a procession of modern-day Lady Godivas parading down Main Street in front of their concerned parents?

I can't leave this subject without going back to Dr. Kellogg. The name probably sounds familiar to you. His family entered the food business. Dismayed by adolescent tastes for spices and other additives, they set out to produce a breakfast cereal that would embody self-restraint and at least ensure the start of the day had a flavor of purity. Cornflakes have continued to cool teenage jets for over a century.

Was all this thinking ridiculous? It's possible I'm being too critical; after all, we get smarter with hindsight. In my defense, I note that prominent writers of the time usually made two claims. The first was that masturbation caused very serious problems, ranging from tuberculosis to insanity. Pictures resembling wanted posters were even published portraying victims of masturbation with glazed eyes and saliva drooling from the corners of their mouths. The second claim was that masturbation was a common problem. If you put these two claims together, the obvious conclusion would be that every time you stepped out of your front door you'd be confronted by hordes of drooling zombies. While there may be times when all of us feel we're surrounded by idiots, we're usually quick to recover a more balanced view of the human race.

People now make jokes about masturbation causing insanity or hair growth on the palms of hands. The recent books on sexuality designed for adolescents will echo this humor. I haven't encountered one that condemns the practice; typically they emphasize that masturbation itself doesn't cause any psychological or physical damage. Yet somehow the high level of fear and anxiety that was so much part of Victorian thinking persists. If you ask teenagers what topics concerning sex they find confusing and would like to know more about, masturbation is high on the list. It's also a subject they find particularly embarrassing to talk about—more so than others, like petting or even intercourse.

The anxiety and embarrassment that continue to accompany the topic of sexuality in our society present obstacles and pitfalls for adolescents. After all, the more embarrassing a subject is, the more people will want to avoid dealing with it openly. But sexuality doesn't simply go away: hormones can't be ignored and the psychological changes in puberty stimulate the sex drive no matter how many cold showers are taken.

GO ASK YOUR FATHER

While teenagers will inevitably try to understand sexuality, they often don't seek information from reliable sources. I grew up in an era when most families and schools avoided the topic of sex. I owe my sex education to my best friend Robert McCauley and the Book Fairy. Robert was a self-proclaimed expert on the topic. The next time I return to England for a visit I want to track him down. Above all, I want to find out if he has a family; from what he told me it would be biologically impossible. Not everyone believes in the Book Fairy, but this is the only explanation I can muster for the book that mysteriously appeared on my dresser one morning when I was an emerging adolescent. It had a green cover; I forget the title, but something like *Everything You Always Wanted to Know About Sex (And Still Won't Know After You Have Finished Reading)* would have been appropriate. Most of it was irrelevant. I learned a lot about how flowers reproduce. If there is reincarnation, don't come back as a daffodil—their sex lives are unbelievably boring. I recall being bitterly disappointed at the absence of pictures, and the description of eggs going down tubes didn't excite me in those days.

Have things changed much? Probably not as much as we'd like to believe. I have occasion in my practice to ask both adults and young people about their sexual histories. I often ask how they obtained information about sex when they were growing up. Almost always their "teachers" were their friends and the schoolyard was the "classroom." It's a law of nature that the less people know about a subject, the more they'll speculate and theorize and eventually begin believing they've discovered the truth. Psychology is living proof of this law. So I continue to meet otherwise intelligent young people who have the strangest beliefs about sex and who are trying very hard, but unsuccessfully, to make sense of the rumors, stories, and "facts" they've heard.

The information young people manage to obtain can have an influence on their behavior. Carol Pardun and her colleagues at the University of North Carolina explored the more subtle messages that come from the media. She noted the frequency of sexual content in the television programs, movies, and magazines popular among teens. For example, over 80 percent of the most popular television shows had sexual content. Only 12 percent, however, had any content relating to sexual risks or responsibilities.

What remained to be determined was the impact of this media diet on behavior. They devised a measure called the Sexual Media Diet based on both the amount of time 12- to 14-year-olds were exposed to the media and the percentage of sexual content. They looked at a broad range of media, including television, movies, magazines, the Internet, and newspapers. Their results indicated that larger consumption of sexual content was associated with both "light" sexual activity, such as French kissing, and "heavy" sexual activity, including intercourse. Consumption also predicted the young person's future intentions to be sexually active.

In the absence of reasoned, well-balanced sex education, it's difficult for our teenagers to make sensible decisions and, while schools have taken a strong role in providing this education, I advocate that parents can be an important source of information and understanding. Every so often a survey is conducted that confirms parents are way down on the list of sources of information about sex. The same type of survey tells us teenagers want more information and wouldn't mind hearing it from us. The topics they'd like on the curriculum include sex drive, masturbation, premarital sexual ethics, orgasm, and birth control.

I have to confess I wasn't very good at teaching my first two children about sex; psychologists have their hang-ups too. The paradox was that I was very comfortable talking to couples and young people about the intimate details of their sex lives during office hours. At home it was a different story, and I conned myself into believing my silence was justified on the grounds I was protecting their innocence.

I've taken a very different approach with my other offspring in the belief that sex education in the home protects children rather than exposes them to risks. We now know that adolescents who receive sex education from their parents are, in fact, somewhat more conservative and responsible regarding sexuality than those who don't. They're less likely to become involved in premarital sexual intercourse, and those girls who do become sexually active are less likely to have an unwanted pregnancy. In general it seems that sex education in the home or school simply doesn't lead to the permissiveness many people feared would follow the "loss of innocence."

I believe adolescents need two types of information. The first is factual and the second has more to do with attitudes, values, and feelings. When it comes to facts, I do recommend books, as well as the videos that are increasingly available. I hasten to add that these shouldn't suddenly appear on your son's or daughter's dresser; this only communicates the idea that his or her emerging sexuality is something to be embarrassed or ashamed about. I always urge parents to review the material first—both as a refresher course for themselves and to ensure the information is clear and acceptable to them given their religious and moral viewpoints. There are many excellent books and videos today that discuss such topics as sexual arousal, erections, menstruation, wet dreams, pimples, masturbation, sexual orientation, differences in breast development, birth control, and sexually transmitted diseases. Some offer humor as well as information. One of my favorite books is *What's Happening to Me?* The cartoon picture of a boy on a diving board looking at two girls and being confronted with a bulge in his swim shorts says it all when it comes to reassuring boys they're not alone if they've found themselves with an unwanted erection.

Some parents I've worked with find the structure of reading a book or watching a video together helps overcome the awkwardness they feel when trying to discuss sex with their children. Quite often it's the same-gender parent who takes on this role, but I don't believe in any hard-and-fast rules about this matter. Being a woman will give a mother an edge when it comes to relating to her daughter's sexuality, and the same obviously applies to fathers and sons. From another perspective, however, being with the opposite-gender parent can reinforce the idea that sexuality can be an open subject in the family rather than taboo.

Safe sex, a topic about which teenagers tell us they'd like to be better informed, is perhaps one of the most important matters for parents to address with their adolescents. The consequences of becoming sexually active can be extremely negative; the most obvious example is AIDS, which has become the deadliest of the sexually transmitted diseases. And each year over a million babies are born in North America as the result of unwanted pregnancies among teenagers. Most of the mothers will keep their babies, and while single teenagers can be excellent parents, many find the task overwhelming and their children suffer as a result. Some will marry because of becoming pregnant, but the likelihood of divorce is very high among this group. Some 40 percent of teenage pregnancies will be terminated by voluntary abortion. For a number of girls this may be experienced as a welcome relief from the stress of pregnancy, but for others it can lead to feelings of guilt and self-reproach they find hard to overcome.

The research I referred to earlier reassures us that giving our children information about safe sex helps them make responsible decisions rather than encouraging them to be sexually active. So give them the straight goods. Remember that almost one-third of younger adolescents believe they can't get pregnant unless they want to. Others believe there are truly safe times during the menstrual cycle (there aren't) or that the withdrawal method guarantees they won't get pregnant (it doesn't).

It's important to add that using scare tactics when discussing safe sex is probably not a good idea. As parents, it's hard not to be afraid for our teenagers. For example, although the likelihood of contracting AIDS is very low in the general population, we can't conclude that it simply couldn't happen to our son or daughter. But social psychologists have long known that if you make people too anxious, they may block out your message. It's likely to be more effective if parents present the information, discuss the risks, and voice their concerns in a serious but relaxed and matter-of-fact manner.

Teens also want a better understanding of homosexuality. We're far from understanding what determines sexual preferences. It used to be thought the way a child was raised determined if she or he would be homosexual. More recently, evidence has come to light that biological/genetic factors may have an important influence. Whatever the reasons, sexual preferences are probably well on their way to being established by the time children enter the teenage years. Young people may, however, find it hard to distinguish this underlying preference from the sexual experimentation with the same gender that can occur in adolescence. For example, over one-third of boys report at least one voluntary homosexual activity that progresses to the point of orgasm. By the time they're entering adulthood, however, over 90 percent of adolescents will have an exclusively heterosexual orientation. This percentage has probably remained the same over the past 50 years.

Along with information about specific topics, it's important to provide a forum for exploring attitudes and values. I usually find it encouraging when I talk to teenagers about how they make decisions about sexual relationships. Whether or not they're sexually active, they typically emphasize issues such as commitment, caring, and respect when they talk about relationships. They may be concerned about pressure to become more sexually active, but the motivation to resist this pressure is often stronger than the desire to conform to other people's expectations.

In my view it can be helpful for even pre-adolescents to be involved in discussions with their parents about how they'll make decisions about sex. Invite them to give you their opinions about when a relationship should include sexual intimacy. Share yours. If you differ, encourage a debate and resist the temptation to lecture that plagues most of us. Ask how young people these days resist pressure. Talk about how you dealt with this issue. Another topic that can be enlightening and enjoyable is gender differences. As much as I hate to admit it, the male of our species does seem to be more primitive when it comes to handling sexual urges. To borrow a line from a movie: "Women need a reason to have sex, men just need a place." In defense of my gender I should add that it seems teenage boys these days place more emphasis on sex being just one part of a relationship than was the case in previous generations. Still, we probably have a long way to go, and a daughter needs to know that she doesn't have to assume any responsibility if her boyfriend becomes overly aroused. If he complains of an ache, she might want to offer a sympathetic sigh, but an icy stare that communicates callous indifference will do just fine.

Fathers can have a particularly strong impact on their sons when dealing with the issue of sexual rights and responsibilities. Date rape is far more common than we once believed. A discussion of how we, as men, are more likely than our partners to allow sexual passion to become sexual coercion and aggression can be very productive. Hopefully, fathers can relate this topic to what has been modeled for years in the home—namely, that power has been shared between the parents without either exercising control through flexing muscles and intimidation.

When adolescents are asked about sexual ethics and morality, they typically stress their right to make their own decisions. There may be times when we need to be directive and impose limits to protect our children from situations we know can be damaging. For the most part, however, I believe our role is to act primarily as consultants to our teenagers. By offering information, encouraging debate, and sharing our own experiences and opinions, we can both respect their right to form their own moral standards and have a positive influence on decisions they do make.

BE HOME BY TEN: THE CHAPERONE NEEDS HER SLEEP

By now I'm sure some of you will have had enough of this general discussion and will want an answer to the following question: "My daughter wants to date and she's not yet 35; what should I do?"

Some families have very definite guidelines. I remember talking to a boy who knew he wouldn't be allowed to date until he was 16. Michael was 14 at the time. He was a delightful lad, and I know he'll become an incurable romantic. He offered no argument with the rule; in fact, he seemed to be capitalizing on it by using the time to plan his first date in great detail and savor the delights of anticipation. The date was scheduled for the evening of his 16th birthday. Michael knew where they'd go and what they'd do. He had rehearsed possible conversations and planned activities that would keep them occupied should there be any awkward moments. I could have kicked myself when I made the completely unnecessary and mundane point that the plan would work only if he actually managed to find someone to go out with him. I felt the guilt deserved by people who burst balloons and rain on parades, and for the next few weeks nothing was said about the topic. Then Michael returned triumphantly with the news that a girl in his class, who was sure she had nothing else booked that day, had promised to be his date. Although I never learned if the big day materialized, I'm sure the fantasy sustained him till he turned 16.

But should a parent set such an arbitrary limit? This is a question I'm asked periodically, and it's hard to answer. As a parent I've never felt the need to set such a limit. Our oldest children didn't seem particularly interested in dating in their early teens. In fact, we were beginning to feel the only way we'd get them off our hands was to emigrate to a country where arranged marriages are still in vogue. Speaking as a psychologist, I always stay where I believe all counselors and therapists should be when it comes to matters of this nature—on the fence. What I will do, however, is discuss several issues related to dating that I think are worth considering.

First of all, what is dating? This may seem an unnecessary question, but the pattern of girlfriend-boyfriend relationships has changed over the past few decades. There's less emphasis on the formal date and more on spending time together in a group that includes both genders. Teenagers don't tend to restrict friendships to the same gender, and they may socialize periodically as a couple without dating as boyfriend and girlfriend. "But he's just a friend" is less likely to be a cover for a secret romance than it was in my generation. Given this pattern of relationships between the sexes, establishing rules can be more difficult. Will your son be permitted to socialize with a female friend as a couple provided it remains strictly platonic? At what point do you consider them to be boyfriend and girlfriend rather than just friends?

Let's assume a relationship has become one of dating rather than just friendship. How concerned should we be? Will our teenagers lose any remnants of reason they had and be ruled entirely by their hormones? It was reassuring for me to read the research I discussed in Chapter Two; this suggests that the majority of adolescents want a lot more than a means of expressing themselves sexually; in fact, most rate the sexual component of a dating relationship as far less important than other aspects of the friendship, such as understanding, affection, and respect.

When we acknowledge both the changes that have taken place in boy-girl relationships in adolescence and the qualities teenagers value in others, we can feel somewhat more confident our sons and daughters will make sensible decisions about dating relationships. Of course, their choices won't always be good ones and they may need our help to avoid or end relationships that are clearly becoming harmful. But their goals for relationships seem commendable.

I believe we often tend to be overly anxious about dating relationships, but I don't advocate a total permissive approach. In keeping with the discussion of parenting styles, I see dating as providing a great opportunity for discussion and negotiation. A first requirement would be an A on the sex education "course" referred to earlier in this chapter. The next step would be to establish guidelines and limits. Do you expect to meet the girlfriend first? How much will you be told about where they're going and with whom? What nights can they go out? How often? Should there be a curfew? Whenever possible I suggest parents raise these questions with their children before they show an interest in dating. This is helpful in two ways. It establishes the expectation that dating, like many other matters, will be discussed and negotiated openly; and it provides reassurance that limits and guidelines will be in place. Dating relationships may be exciting, but they can also be a source of anxiety and pressure. Knowing that parents will retain some degree of control can avoid the anxiety and stress that having too much freedom too quickly can bring.

And while we're on the topic of anxiety and stress, the subject of dating is a must for sharing your own experiences. For many of us the prospect of dating fed into our worst fears as well as our favorite fantasies. Being turned down, not knowing what to say, and having to coat yourself with antiperspirant before you even thought about engineering a first kiss aren't exactly treasured moments. But I'm a great believer in getting as much mileage as possible out of the painful lessons of our past, and I have a veritable wealth of non-experiences to draw on when it comes to dating. Without knowing it, I must have had a way of communicating over the telephone that ensured girls wouldn't feel worried or pressured by any reluctance to reject me. They turned me down without so much as a moment's thought, and most didn't even have the decency to stifle their laughter. But after allowing my bruised ego to recover, I'd try again, knowing that sooner or later I'd catch someone off guard and get the arrangements made before they came to their senses. So eventually Joan became my first girlfriend, and I know to this day that deep in her heart she truly loved me, even though word got back after we broke up that she thought I was a lousy kisser. What really hurt was that she told everyone exactly why I was such a lousy kisser. Being in a state of near panic, I apparently shook and trembled so hard that it was like kissing a jackhammer.

Teenagers sometimes don't know their parents have had to deal with the same concerns, heartaches, fears, and disappointments they face. I encourage my children to see the humor in their father's struggles as an adolescent in the hope they'll be more accepting of theirs.

CHAPTER 8

GIRLS AND BOYS

My search of one of the main databases in psychology netted over 11,000 journal articles on the topic of gender differences in childhood and adolescence. Researchers have taken on the challenge of trying to tease apart the effects of biology and those of socialization. The finding that boys are more physically aggressive than girls may not be the result of innate gender differences—it could reflect the fact that we still raise girls to be the "gentler sex." Similarly, a number of studies have found that boys score higher on math tests. It's possible the male brain comes pre-wired for math, but it could also be the case that we encourage boys more than girls to achieve in math.

I'm glad I didn't have the daunting task of reading all 11,000 articles before forming an opinion on the matter. Fortunately, the research has been reviewed and summarized by a number of scholars, and the conclusion is that the notion of gender differences has been grossly exaggerated. I wouldn't have made this statement before reading "The Gender Similarities Hypothesis" in *American Psychologist*. Its author, Janet Shibley Hyde of the University of Wisconsin, analyzed 46 reviews; in combination, these reviews had examined over 4,300 studies. A wide range of possible gender differences had been considered, including cognitive abilities, self-esteem, social and personality characteristics, motor behavior, and moral reasoning. She concluded that, for the most part, the genders are similar and when differences are found, these are small and unlikely to be of much significance. There are a few exceptions—males can outdo females on certain motor tasks such as throwing a ball for distance, they masturbate more frequently, and they are more aggressive. I'd contend that two of the three fall into the "do we really care or want to know" category.

Hyde draws attention to the cost of inflated claims of gender differences. We're told women and men are so unalike they might as well have originated from different planets. Making such an assumption could lead to the belief that conflict is inevitable, and there's little point trying to understand or communicate with the opposite gender. Purported differences in cognitive skills lead to erroneous assumptions about who's better suited for a particular occupation, and unsupported claims that males are less empathic and caring can reinforce the myth they're less competent as all-round parents.

After many decades of research, we're left with the conclusion that the genders are far more alike with respect to their abilities and other characteristics than has been asserted in the past. That doesn't, of course, mean their roles have been similar. Socialization is a major force to be reckoned with. Girls are taught to be girls and boys to be boys. Presumably the family has an impact, but so would the child's experiences at school. And what about the books they read and the television programs and movies they watch? Like it or not, girls and women remain under-represented as the heroes and otherwise competent and appealing characters in fiction.

I've restricted myself to discussing a few topics that will be of particular interest to parents of teenagers. These topics relate to a single question: what can we do to reduce the likelihood that gender stereotypes will limit our teenagers' potential to achieve success and satisfaction in the areas they value the most—education, career, family life, and relationships?

WE *HAVE* COME A LONG WAY

A brief look at history should leave no doubt that society's values, beliefs, and expectations have placed unnecessary and oppressive restrictions on both genders—especially girls. The industrial revolution created a demand for a highly educated work force. This, together with the high infant mortality rate, led to the need for large families. For well over a century it was almost universally accepted that the responsibility for meeting these two needs would be assigned strictly according to gender: men worked outside the home and women raised the children.

The fact that boys were destined to work outside the home made them obvious candidates for an educational system that could prepare them for competitive employment. But girls were a different story. The assumption that their destiny centered on hearth and home may have been challenged in some quarters, but it was firmly ingrained in the culture at large.

Theorists at the time were quick to justify the separation of the genders. Girls were made differently; their innate differences were a fact of life, and no one should mess with Nature's design. Experts argued that girls were short more than a few neurons when it came to higher learning. Although smart enough to write *The Daughters of England* in the early Victorian era, Sara Ellis subscribed to this view of the female capacity to learn and achieve: "As women then, the first thing of importance is to be content to be inferior to men—inferior in mental power in the same proportion as you are inferior in body strength." If this line of reasoning didn't leave you totally convinced, you were reminded that the Virgin Mary, who would be the undisputed role model for any girl, "knew nothing of letters." The fact that Joseph might not have scored that well on tests of reading or spelling was conveniently ignored.

For the more enlightened, the emphasis on gender roles didn't have to mean girls were destined to become no more than illiterate housekeepers. No man would want to come home to a wife whose horizons didn't extend beyond cooking, cleaning, and laundry. Although these activities might indeed occupy most of her day, the woman should at least know something of the broader world from which she was excluded. There was, therefore, an agreement that girls should be schooled. Literature and the arts were appropriate and a smattering of history and geography wouldn't hurt. But technical subjects and the sciences were a different matter. These had no relevance to performing domestic duties and were, in any case, too complex for the female mind.

For many Victorian advice-givers, the onset of puberty was the time to ensure that gender role training was undertaken with renewed vigor. As physical differentiation became more pronounced, so did the awareness that girls and boys were supposed to be headed in different directions. The Laws of Nature were indisputable—too much education of the mind would be at the expense of the body. Experts wrote extensively on the topic of women's inherently weaker constitutions and spoke with authority about the risk that studying demanding subjects, such as math, would cause the uterus to atrophy and inhibit breast development. If that wasn't sufficient to deter young women from pursuing higher education, then fear of insanity could be evoked. Proof was offered. Women in asylums were more likely to be educated than were male patients; the brainwork had simply been too much for their feeble minds.

THE CONTINUING LEGACY

The obvious contrasts between our beliefs and practices today and those of the Victorian era tell us that much progress has been made in ensuring girls have the opportunity to succeed in education and employment. But there continue to be ways in which parents may unwittingly reinforce gender stereotypes. My oldest daughter is in her thirties. I remember confessing to her that I'd felt more concerned about her younger brother's education than hers. Intellectually I knew that education was just as important for Joanne, and I believe we gave her just as much support and encouragement as her brother. But I grew up in an era when there seemed to be less need for young women to be highly educated, as it was assumed their primary mission in life was to be full-time homemakers. Old beliefs die hard and studies of child-rearing values continue to indicate that gender-bias has an influence. For example, parents are more likely to place high value on achievement and competitiveness for their teenage sons, while warmth and compliance are priorities for their daughters.

Observations of parents and adolescents performing tasks also reveal significant differences. Parents appear to demand greater independence from boys; while they're quick to give assistance to girls, they stand back and allow the boys to wrestle with the problem. This wish to "rescue" girls probably accounts for the finding that both parents and teachers are likely to interrupt girls more than boys during conversations about a variety of topics. They also wait longer for boys to answer questions than girls. This lack of confidence that girls will be able to figure things out for themselves can be unconscious and can influence people even when they're committed to being fair and equitable. It serves as a reminder of the need to be vigilant in the way we relate to the genders. I have a good friend who's a teacher; she's determined to avoid this bias and makes sure she always gives both her female and male students a mental count of 10 to answer questions in class.

The research is clear: girls have no difficulty holding their own on tests of intelligence and have consistently demonstrated that the earlier belief in their inferior learning potential was without foundation. Most of us are probably aware of this finding and have long accepted that girls and boys don't differ in their overall intelligence. The risk that we'll nonetheless have different expectations according to gender is illustrated by the finding that parents tend to attribute low achievement in daughters to lack of ability; sons who aren't working up to snuff are more likely to be seen as "goofing off." Similarly, studies have shown that female students may be rated as less capable by their teachers, even when their achievement equals that of their male classmates.

I find it encouraging to read studies that fly in the face of conventional wisdom. I was interested to come across a report from an engineering program in England. Contrary to the expectation that prevailed at the time, the young women were graduating with slightly higher marks in their math courses than their male peers (presumably they were unaware they were supposed to come in second). As far as we know, they also escaped any major damage to their figures and fertility.

These findings are of more than academic interest. Many studies tell us that parents' beliefs about gender differences in specific abilities are powerful. For example, parents' assumptions that their daughters are stronger in English while their sons are better at math can exist even when there's no actual disparity in the level of achievement. The starting point appears to be the extent to which parents assume the genders are innately distinct with respect to abilities. The more this belief is held, the greater is the likelihood that parents will assume their children's potential will be enhanced or limited by this factor. The chain reaction continues: the parents' expectations have the power to influence how their children will evaluate their own potential, which, in turn, can influence their motivation, effort, and achievement.

The value of the research is that it highlights ways in which parents can take steps to reduce the impact of negative expectations. The more we remind ourselves of the need to rid ourselves of gender bias in our thinking, the better able we become to form our expectations on the basis of our children's real, rather than assumed, potential. Professor Laura Beck's review of the literature led her to state, "Our overall conclusion must be that males and females are more alike in developmental potential than they are different from each other." Through our expectations, comments, and words of encouragement, we have tremendous power to communicate this conclusion to our daughters and sons.

ARE THE TABLES BEING TURNED?

The more recent findings from studies of educational achievement support the view that the earlier tendency for girls to underestimate and underutilize their potential is diminishing. Objective measures of their achievement at high school and in postsecondary education indicate a declining gender gap. In fact, women are just as likely to graduate from university as men, and in North America they go on to obtain slightly more than half of all degrees at the master's level. Reading these findings reminded me of a recent experience at a university graduation. As much as all of us in the audience tried to feign unbridled enthusiasm, I didn't notice anyone taping the three-and-a-half-hour ceremony in order to save it for their viewing pleasure. Kathy and I were eventually reduced to reading the program for entertainment. While this did little to alleviate the tedium, we were interested to note that most of the awards for academic excellence had been earned by women.

Signs that boys may be lagging behind girls in certain areas have prompted some writers to discuss the possible impact of a negative male subculture. One recent study found that teenage girls reported greater personal involvement in school; they also valued academic success more highly. Perhaps it's not "cool" for older boys to focus too much on schoolwork; to do so would put them at risk of being labeled a "geek." This type of peer pressure is less influential for girls, and this factor, together with their growing awareness of their potential, encourages continuing achievement as they approach adulthood.

GLASS CEILINGS AND GLASS WALLS

Education has value in its own right, but it's also nice to know it can help you get a job you'll find enjoyable, worthwhile, and financially rewarding. Ideally, the range of occupations open to our children and their chances for advancement in these occupations will be determined by their abilities and potential, not their gender. I hope my optimism regarding the positive trends in this area won't prove to be naive. Much depends on how you care to describe the statistics. It's true that women are under-represented in fields such as engineering, law, skilled trades, and medicine. But it's also true that over the past three decades women have successfully broken through these "glass walls," establishing an increasing presence in these and other male-dominated occupations. One particularly encouraging statistic is that in 1999 there were more women than men graduating from medical school in Canada. The same optimistic outlook can be applied to the "glass ceilings" that have excluded women from rising to the more senior positions in fields such as commerce, industry, and education; there's no doubt that advancement remains harder for women than should be the case, but upward mobility isn't as difficult as it has been historically.

There are ways in which gender stereotypes are especially restrictive for boys. Girls may be predisposed to be less active and competitive, but this hasn't stopped them from growing up to excel in traditionally male territory. It appears, however, that we're less willing to allow boys to relinquish the traditional masculine role. As mentioned previously, the pressure to conform to this role is strong and comes not only from parents but also from peers and the boys themselves. As a consequence, boys may be less motivated to even try to penetrate the barriers.

I supervised a student whose research looked at under-graduates' perceptions of how suitable occupations were for their own gender. There were no indications of gender bias among the women. For example, traditionally male occupations such as mechanic or pilot were rated highly. The male students, however, were influenced by gender stereotypes; on average, they rated occupational choices such as nursing and nursery school teacher less favorably than traditionally male sectors of the work force. This gender difference had nothing to do with the student's per-ception of the socioeconomic status of the respective occupations; the young men made gender-stereotypic choices even when they rated the occupations as being of equal status in society.

Parents again emerge as a powerful instrument for change. While we are by no means the sole determinants of our children's vocational aspirations, I find it reassuring that we do help shape their more important values. Parents who believe girls and boys should have equal access to all sectors of the work force and who communicate this attitude through what they say and do have a reasonable chance of passing this value on to their adolescents.

BOYS WILL BE BOYS?

Long before toddlers have the cognitive skills needed to comprehend that there are two genders, they play in ways that conform to the prevailing stereotypes. By the age of 18 months boys will show a preference for toys that allow them to be active, such as cars and trucks. This preference is demonstrable even when parents have taken care to provide a variety of toys—the dolls simply aren't on the list of preferred activities. The reverse holds true for little girls, who are more likely to engage in less rambunctious activities that communicate caring and affection. By the age of three or four, gender-specific play is very easy to observe when choices are available. Furthermore, children are beginning to develop a definite understanding of what are "correct" activities for boys and girls.

These early differences have frequently been studied in the context of the development of male aggression and its effects on boys' ability to deal appropriately with the conflicts and disputes that inevitably arise in relationships. The vast majority of physically aggressive acts in our society are committed by males, and the incidents of random and unprovoked killings by adolescent boys in high schools have heightened concerns that their propensity for violence is a serious problem in our society.

One perspective starts with the notion that biology dictates the male of the species is far more active. There's a body of evidence to support this view. For example, little boys all over the world engage in far more rough-and-tumble play than little girls; the same is true for many other infant male primates, such as chimpanzees. I have no quarrel with this theory. I've had the opportunity to supervise many groups of small children, and the differences in activity levels aren't hard to notice. As much as I try to repress the memory, I can't forget the experience of taking some 20 primary boys on a tour of a local television studio. I knew we were headed for disaster the moment the manager took them into the control room and told them not to touch any of the countless buttons and levers beckoning from the panels and screens.

Innate differences in activity level may, in turn, predispose boys to become more competitive and subsequently more physical in the way they deal with conflict. One longitudinal study found that boys who became involved in the more vigorously competitive types of sports and recreational activities were rated by others as being the more aggressive members of their peer group. This difference hadn't been present before the boys' involvement in these activities.

The disparity in levels of physical aggression between the genders increases with age, suggesting the role of environmental influences. The expectation that boys will be more competitive and assertive is present in many cultures, as is the expectation that girls will be more caring and demure. In addition, the research tells us the pressure on boys to conform to the masculine stereotype is stronger than the corresponding pressure for girls. By the time they reach adolescence, boys don't experience as much guilt as girls when they are physically aggressive. They're also less prosocial in their values, placing less emphasis on altruism than girls; this disparity increases over the teenage years.

I should add that teenage girls aren't truly "sugar and spice and all things nice." While they still commit fewer acts of violence than boys, they can be very aggressive. They express their anger differently, however, using strategies such as malicious gossip and isolating the offending party from their social group. When this type of behavior is taken into consideration, the frequency of aggression among girls equals that of boys. The obvious distinction is that male aggression is far more likely to lead to socially unacceptable and illegal ways of coping with anger and provocation.

The possibility that the gender gap with respect to aggression is decreasing has to be considered. At first glance, the numbers would support this hypothesis: the difference in the number of charges for violent offenses between girls and boys has declined. Such a trend, however, could be the result of other factors. One has been referred to as the "chivalry hypothesis." Perhaps we were reluctant in the past to charge girls for behavior that was traditionally seen as male or too quick to assume they were acting in self-defense. The nature of the charges also has to be taken into account. Boys are still more likely to commit the more serious violent crimes; just comparing the overall numbers fails to reflect this important difference.

The topic of aggression provides another opportunity to extol the virtues of the democratic parenting style. There's no simple relationship between parenting style and aggression; there's also some evidence that rigid, confrontational approaches to discipline can result from—rather than cause—children's aggressive behavior. At the same time, the way in which parents model how to exercise power and cope with conflict is a critical factor. A major goal of democratic parenting is to provide children with the opportunity to grow up in an atmosphere of mutual respect where conflicts lead to communication and negotiation rather than warfare.

Lori D'Angelo studied the effects of living in a home environment that doesn't offer such an opportunity. Her master's thesis research looked specifically at the father's influence. In her article "Like Father, Like Son?" published in *Developmental Psychology*, she describes the "robust association" between the fathers' levels of self-restraint as measured when their sons were age 12 and the boys' subsequent behavior on reaching 16. Fathers who were prone to exhibiting poor self-control and whose behavior was aggressive and inconsiderate of others were likely to have sons who displayed comparable characteristics four years later. Similarly, other studies tell us that when conflicts between parents lead to verbal or physical aggression, sons are far more likely than daughters to develop similar patterns of behavior. Finally, a combination of authoritarian, coercive child-rearing and lack of supervision outside the home places boys at particularly high risk for becoming involved in negative peer groups that condone and reinforce aggression.

MR. MOM (AND MRS. DAD?)

Parents also have an important part to play in determining how their sons and daughters will approach family life. The tenacity of the masculine stereotype can deny boys tremendous opportunities for growth and satisfaction. Let me return briefly to the opposite gender. Women who have children but who are also heavily invested in their education and occupations don't typically place their careers ahead of their family life; they rate both as their highest priorities. Women are onto something. It wasn't that childcare was so aversive; it was more a case of being denied the chance to expand their range of activities beyond hearth and home. The role descriptions for girls have been expanded, not reversed; to my knowledge, no one is advocating that "caring" and "nurturing" should be struck off the list.

As yet, however, it seems we've fallen behind in our efforts to teach boys their lives will be enriched if they, too, expand their role descriptions. I want to be careful not to overstate my case. I have firsthand knowledge of the mundane aspects of childcare and housework; the fact that I no longer have any nose to wipe other than my own brings no great sadness, and I don't consider the opportunity to do dishes with my children as an irreplaceable bonding experience. But I challenge you to name something more rewarding than holding your smiling infant while he falls asleep or watching your daughter beam with pride and pleasure as she performs in a school concert.

The belief in innate differences in parenting ability remains a formidable obstacle to encouraging boys to redefine their future role in family life. The argument that the male of the species lacks the gene needed to change diapers and clean toilets may not be tenable, but the assumption that fathers and mothers have distinct roles is central to the thinking of some childcare writers. Not long ago an article in a popular parenting magazine discussed how both parents have important but complementary roles. The psychologist asserted that because of the "invisible emotional umbilical cord" mothers are better equipped to provide the closeness and comfort their children need. Fathers, on the other hand, become involved in parenting "in a masculine way"—for example, allowing children more freedom so they can develop independence and being more consistent with respect to discipline.

This gender stereotyping is countered by the increasing number of studies that led one reviewer to conclude that "men have at least the potential to be as good caretakers of children as women are." Observations of parent-child interactions demonstrate that fathers can be just as nurturing toward their children; they're equally as responsive to their infants' vocalizations and movements and respond just as quickly to a baby's signs of distress. Similarly, mothers aren't adept only at communicating affection and sensitivity toward their children but are equally as effective in the "masculine" domains of parenting. The influence of expectations and socialization rather than biology is again evident; the lack of difference between the way in which mothers and fathers interact with their children is most frequently found in countries such as Sweden, where there's a longer history of support for shared parenting.

We may be behind, but I'm confident we're getting there. A recent newspaper report of nontraditional career days for teenagers illustrated both the progress and the distance yet to be traveled. Parents at the school had pointed out that the previous career days had been designed to encourage the girls to be broader in their thinking. As a result, the invitation list was restricted to women who worked in traditionally male occupations. The parents had sought a more balanced approach, and the list was extended to include men who worked in traditionally female occupations. Also invited was a full-time male homemaker, a clear message to our teenage sons that being a full-time homemaker and parent can be just as valid a choice for them as it is for girls. My only complaint was this particular workshop was entitled "Mr. Mom," unintentionally implying yet again that males who take on domestic roles are crossing over into foreign territory. My hope is that we'll soon reach the point where we're no more inclined to refer to men who participate equally in family life as "Mr. Mom" than we are to refer to women who participate equally in the work force as "Mrs. Dad."

A FEW REMINDERS TO OURSELVES

An exercise I've introduced in workshops asks parents to discuss and list ways in which we can encourage our teens to combine the positive aspects of both traditional gender stereotypes. I like to emphasize the small, subtle ways in which gender biases can be reinforced. I doubt many parents spend much time discussing gender stereotypes with their daughters and sons; these can nonetheless be communicated by facets of everyday life that, while sometimes seeming trivial in isolation, have a cumulative effect on how young people think and act. A last point I make is that, even when parents truly want their children to be free of gender biases, their own past experiences and enduring habits may unintentionally lead them to reinforce the stereotypes.

Over the years I've compiled a checklist based on the parents' responses. As a parent, I've found the list a useful way to remind myself of the need to pay close attention to how we relate to our own children.

- **Is the distribution of chores and responsibilities free of bias?** If boys can operate a lawn mower there's no reason why they couldn't learn to be in charge of a washer and drier, and vice versa for girls. Cooking, dishes, putting out the garbage, taking care of younger siblings, and cleaning are other examples of activities that should provide equal opportunity for resistance and complaint.

- **When there are two parents in the home, are chores and responsibilities also free of bias?** This doesn't mean all tasks should be divided equally between parents. I've never had any desire to appeal Kathy's ruling that I'm not permitted in the laundry room, but she knows better than to mess with my kitchen.

- **If you could see a videotape of your family in the community, would there be any signs that leadership is assigned to the father?** Who drives the car and pumps the gas; who places the order or pays the bill in a restaurant?

- **Are boys encouraged to participate in activities that foster cooperation and nonaggressive competition?** I'm not hinting at a ban on the forms of competitive sport that require physical force, such as hockey and football; what I'd advocate, however, is that we also steer them in the direction of equally challenging activities that don't require this type of aggression—for example, swimming, baseball, cycling, and track and field.

- **Are girls encouraged to participate in competitive team activities?** Girls are more likely to be directed toward forms of individual competition like figure skating and gymnastics. Team sports such as hockey or soccer can provide opportunities to learn how to combine cooperation and competitiveness.

- **Do you argue constructively and safely with your spouse?** (If your marriage has remained in a state of perpetual bliss and you've never so much as considered exchanging a cross word, could you pretend to have an argument just for the children's sake?) Use disputes and differences of opinion as opportunities for children to learn that conflict can lead to resolving matters in a way that doesn't involve one gender dominating and controlling the other.

- **Do you communicate expectations regarding school work that are based on ability not gender?** Not all students can achieve at the same level and everyone has areas of relative strength and weakness, but gender itself doesn't have to be a significant factor.

- **Although day-to-day experiences are probably more influential than abstract discussions, do you try to stimulate the occasional debate on gender issues?** It can be interesting to find out the extent to which teenagers feel there are real differences in ability or appropriate roles. It can be even more interesting to challenge their views and assumptions—remembering, of course, to listen carefully to their opinions without interrupting daughters any more than sons.

- Is it likely your children believe that, in addition to sharing household tasks, you view their upbringing as a joint responsibility? Are both parents as equally involved in their lives as schedules permit? Is it always one parent who takes them shopping, helps them with homework, goes to school interviews and open houses, exercises discipline, and takes care of doctors' appointments? Single mothers obviously have much less opportunity to demonstrate that child-rearing can be shared, but they can include this area in discussions with their children. Asking their teenage sons what type of father they'd like to be if they decide to have a family at least introduces the idea that the question "what do you want to do when you grow up?" doesn't refer only to employment outside the home.

- Do you discuss employment options in a way that cuts across traditional gender lines? By the time our children reach their teens we've often acquired definite ideas about their strengths and weaknesses. This awareness can prompt discussion about areas they might want to explore as possible career choices. But are your suggestions about careers based on their abilities or have they been determined partially by what you consider to be masculine or feminine occupations?

I have no desire to take the spontaneity out of family life. It would be tedious, oppressive, and somewhat absurd to maintain a schedule of whose turn it is to drive the car or insist that your son be allowed to join the local synchronized swimming team while his sister dons a football uniform. But the attitudes we communicate in our day-to-day interactions with our children do make a difference. The way in which we relate to the opposite gender and our approach to raising our daughters and sons affords us an opportunity to counteract the limitations of traditional stereotypes.

CHAPTER 9

SCHOOL, WORK, AND PLAY

We have a son whose body contours match perfectly to those of couches and armchairs. By Saturday afternoon we often feel the need to give him a poke to upgrade his condition from coma to semi-stupor. Once we get him up and doing something he has energy to spare; left to his own devices, however, he'd soon view operating the channel changer as forced labor.

One important part of children's development is to reach the point where they no longer rely on others to energize and direct them. Children seem to acquire these internal controls at different rates, and a common concern for parents is that their son or daughter isn't showing the drive and motivation needed to achieve success.

SCHOOL: LEADING HORSES TO WATER

It would be hard not to have liked Mark. This 16-year-old boy had an easy, pleasant manner and a keen sense of humor. He obviously had a relaxed attitude to life, and this was driving his parents to distraction. Each semester his typical pattern was to coast for the first couple of months, warm up very slowly after experiencing the fallout from his midsemester report card, and then work with modest enthusiasm to ensure that he at least passed some of his courses. His parents were frustrated because they were certain he could achieve higher grades. They also knew that unless his marks improved, his chances of being accepted at a college or university would be negligible, and they wanted him to have this option.

Parents often share this type of concern regarding school achievement, and understandably so. It continues to be the case that the higher the level of education reached, the better are the young person's prospects in the work force. While there's some truth to the idea that there has been a glut of college graduates in certain fields, the unemployment rate for those who complete postsecondary education remains lower than for those who don't. One factor is the shifting pattern in the demand for different types of occupations. For example, the number of jobs available to semiskilled industrial and farm workers has declined and is expected to continue to do so. The need for people with technical and professional qualifications, however, has increased in many areas.

Mark's parents wanted to know what to do. Their question was simple: "How do we get him to work?" I've been asked this question in various forms by many parents, and I dread it. "Beats me" or "That's a really good question—I wish I knew the answer" are responses that don't enhance my reputation. When confronted with this issue, I suggest a checklist the parents might use to determine if there are additional steps that could be taken to support and direct their teenager's education.

Number one on my list is the question of determining realistic expectations for school performance. Mark's parents saw him as bright and so they were convinced he could do well if only he'd work harder. In most instances parents have no reason to question their judgment, but situations can arise in which the expectations for young people exceed their potential. It's hard to discuss this matter without touching on several issues, each of which could occupy a full book. What I'll try to do, however, is take a position I hope will at least come close to one that's acceptable. I do believe there are innate differences in intelligence: some children are quicker to learn than others. Of course, the quality of the environment—and in particular, the extent to which parents and teachers stimulate and challenge the child—will have a very important role. But it's still the case that for some children learning comes more easily.

We tend not to make the distinctions between children in terms of their intelligence that we did several years ago. Whatever terms were actually used, this early categorization of children sadly left some feeling slow or stupid, while others thought of themselves as the cream of the crop. We're now far less inclined to label children. We're also less prone to failing them in elementary school as the research tells us that repeating a grade is likely to have a detrimental effect on long-term achievement. One consequence is that, by the middle school years, there can be a very large range in abilities among the students in a particular grade. It wouldn't, for example, be at all unusual to find a grade eight class in which there's a student who can read as well as most adults and another who's barely literate. As a consequence, grade placement may not reflect the actual level of achievement.

My suggestion to Mark and his parents was that it would be helpful to postpone meeting as a family and arrange individual testing sessions to obtain a profile of his abilities and potential. Like most young people, Mark enjoyed this process and, at the end of all the tests of intelligence, memory, aptitudes, and interest patterns, I was able to give him a reasonable picture of his relative strengths and weaknesses. This type of information can be useful when planning both a high school program and considering possible career directions.

I had to break the news to Mark that he did well on the testing. I told him I had no choice but to tell his parents he was not only quite bright but also possessed an excellent memory. These findings would only confirm their view that he was underachieving. We discussed a possible bribe. For a modest sum I could tell his parents that his potential was unfortunately limited in the hope that they would no longer harass him about school work, but we were unable to agree on terms, so the truth was revealed.

But not all students end up with profiles like Mark's. Over the years I've seen a number of young people whose intellectual and memory skills are below average and who are trying to contend with course work that's just too difficult for them. A student taking grade 11 advanced courses whose intellectual potential and basic academic skills are in the bottom 25 percent of her age group will almost inevitably find it very hard, if not impossible, to obtain acceptable marks. When discussing such results I raise the difficult but important issue of revising expectations for achievement. Obviously we want to avoid selling students short by setting expectations too low; if young people are led to believe they can't reach a certain goal, this lack of confidence can lead to their failing to achieve in situations where success might, in fact, be possible. At the same time, if expectations are too high, the frustration associated with feeling overwhelmed by school work and experiencing repeated failures can damage self-esteem severely and foster increasingly negative attitudes toward education. Some middle ground needs to be established so students can use the skills they have and experience success. This may mean taking a reduced academic load or transferring to courses that are less academically demanding.

I should also mention specific learning disabilities. Students with such disabilities are of at least average intelligence and some are very bright. For reasons we don't yet understand adequately, however, they have a specific area of weakness that interferes with their progress. This "learning block" can create a puzzling picture. Kim began avoiding school in grade eight. Her first approach was to develop aches and pains and use these to persuade her parents to let her stay home. When this strategy was no longer effective, she began refusing to hand in assignments and occasionally taking off from school without permission. Kim's report card typically indicated that her rate of progress was slow and that she had particular difficulty with written work. Just talking to Kim, however, was sufficient to tell you she was bright. She used her extensive vocabulary articulately, and it came as no surprise to learn from her teachers that, in spite of her academic difficulties, she could be a star in classroom discussions.

Kim did very well on the intellectual assessment. It was painful for all concerned, however, to give her the test of writing skills. The girl who had no difficulty holding her own in conversations with adults couldn't construct a sentence or spell words that had been part of her spoken vocabulary for years.

Kim's learning disability was in the areas of symbolic language and visual-motor integration. All these terms mean is that she had specific weakness connecting sounds to letters, as well as difficulty with the mechanics of printing and writing. For Kim and her parents, knowing the problem was due to a learning disability came as a great relief. Kim wasn't underachieving; she wasn't lazy and the owner of a bad attitude. She was a bright person with a disability that was no one's fault. Now an effort could be made to develop a program consistent with her learning disability, such as including more oral examination, providing remedial tutoring, and teaching her how to take advantage of technology such as word processing, voice-to-text software, and programs that would scan and read material to her.

The second item on the list is to explore study skills. Some students seem to develop these naturally; others don't. Two of our children are perfect illustrations. Kiera organizes her notes, starts working on assignments in plenty of time, and plans when to study before a test. Aaron is a different story. Our greatest fear is that the state of his notebooks might reflect the state of his mind. He swears he was the only student in his high school never to have been given an examination schedule or more than 12 hours notice that essays and projects are due.

While achievement is still valued highly in North America, our study habits generally seem weak in comparison to other cultures. For many European and Japanese students, for example, three to four hours of homework a night isn't unusual. By comparison, the results from one North American study tell us that less than one-third of students spend an average of an hour or more studying each night. Forty percent report they typically do no homework whatsoever.

Many students get by for years with poor study habits and skills. Sooner or later, however, they may find their natural intelligence is no longer sufficient to get them through. They need to become more organized and efficient but lack the skills to do so. I like to ask students what approaches they use to taking notes from classes or books and how far in advance they set up a timetable for studying. Blank stares are far more common than answers and make it clear that foreign concepts are being introduced. This can promote a discussion about how the necessary skills could be acquired. There are excellent books and programs on the market that make study skills quite easy to learn and apply. Libraries, bookstores, the Internet, and especially guidance departments at high schools are all potential resources for information and materials. And parents can help provide the structure that may be needed by younger high school students. Negotiations regarding how much time your son and daughter should set aside for studying each night may be long overdue. If they protest and start to claim you're robbing them of their childhood, threaten them with boarding school in Tokyo or Geneva.

As for number three on the list, I advise a modified version of the "don't you know the value of an education" lecture. I emphasize that it should be a *modified* version; in its standard, unabridged form it's likely to evoke only eye-rolling, sighs, and passive indifference. And tailor the discussion to the teenager's aspirations. You can rest assured that most adolescents have the types of goals and ambitions that would meet with their parents' approval; several studies have indicated that young people's job aspirations either reflect or surpass their parents' level of achievement. It also seems to be the case that these aspirations remain fairly consistent. If their goals do become more modest, it's usually because the students become more realistic—for example, acknowledging that a career in engineering is probably not feasible if math is a relatively weak subject.

So the typical problem isn't one of an absence of goals but rather lack of information regarding how they might be achieved. When students don't have information it can be hard for them to truly appreciate how important their performance in their current courses may or may not be. For example, I've talked to young people who don't understand that obtaining papers for the skilled trades often requires passing fairly tough examinations as well as gaining practical experience. I've also met other students who don't realize that law involves postgraduate training, which requires an undergraduate degree that, in turn, requires getting the level of marks needed to enter university. The object, therefore, is to inform young people so they can reach their own opinions about the value of an education. Some parents will be able to provide their daughter or son with the type of information they need. Many won't: it's hard to keep abreast of changes in the educational system or to know what jobs are out there and how to qualify for them. This is where career counseling comes in, and many see this as a process that should start early in high school.

When discussing career counseling, I emphasize that the objective isn't to slot teenagers into particular occupations but to give them the facts needed to become aware of how their current choice of courses and level of achievement can influence the range of careers open to them as they reach adulthood. One study involving over 32,000 high school students found that two-thirds of eleventh graders had never received any career guidance. This situation seems to be changing for the better, but it may still be necessary for parents and their teenagers to take the initiative in obtaining counseling through the high school guidance department, career counseling services in the community, or their own research, using materials available in the career sections of libraries and bookstores.

The fourth and last item on the checklist focuses on teenagers' emotional well-being. Are there family difficulties that are interfering with school? For example, it's hard for students to concentrate on their work if they're worried that their parents might be splitting up. Is a girl chronically unhappy because of problems with peers? Could a boy's avoidance of school be related to drug or alcohol abuse? If it seems that difficulties of this nature are present, the question becomes not so much one of getting the young person to work but addressing the problems that stop them from working. This can require family or individual counseling or other mental health services.

So let's say your daughter is bright enough to succeed, has appropriate study skills (or the opportunity to acquire them), is aware that 50 percent in grade nine Latin won't guarantee a place in medical school, and is as psychologically stable as her age and your spouse's family background will permit. What steps can you now take if she continues to be on strike at school? Referring back to that old saying about horses and water, perhaps there comes a time when you have to acknowledge that the water is there in plenty and you've done all the leading possible. The last step isn't one for you to take.

My mother decided I was a horse when I was 16. After lamenting that the law forbade her to send me to the glue factory, she acknowledged I'd have to find out for myself that an education is important. Eventually it did become extremely important to me, but that was after several years and many jobs.

I'm always careful about sharing my history with families. First of all, they haven't come to see me because of any interest in my life. Furthermore, I don't want to convey the message that leaving school at 16 is a good idea. At the same time, once young people have an awareness of their potential and have the opportunity to use this, parents have, in my opinion, done their job and done it well. If their son or daughter is of school-leaving age and continues to use high school as a cross between a drop-in center and a retirement home, I ask them to consider employment as an alternative to education. I can fully appreciate why parents are often reluctant to do this. They know that not having a high school diploma will be a significant obstacle to finding more than a menial, low-paying job. But staying at school and doing next to nothing doesn't exactly prepare a teenager for the work force, and it may even teach her that being clothed, fed, and watered is her birthright and that she has to do absolutely nothing in return. Most young people will develop sufficient self-motivation to sustain them through high school and beyond. For those who don't, I believe little can be accomplished by nagging them repeatedly.

Mark left high school at 17 without a diploma. I continued to meet with the family intermittently after the decision to leave school had been made. We deliberately used the term "leaving" school, not "quitting" or "dropping out." Mark was going to try something else, and his parents were there to offer support and encouragement. Mark's task was a hard one. It took a lot of searching to find work, and after paying for room and board, all his clothing, and other necessities, he wasn't enjoying the lifestyle he wanted. Although it was difficult, his parents continued to support his decision and decided never to say anything close to "We told you it wasn't easy out there." While enduring deep teeth marks on their tongues was painful at times, they concentrated on what Mark was achieving, knowing how important it would be that they not see him as a failure and communicate this view to him.

I'll have to disappoint those of you who are waiting for a happy ending. I don't know if Mark ever decided to return to school, although he still has very many years to continue his education if he so chooses. As we'd discussed with him, brain cells don't rot—at least not for many decades past your teens. If it becomes important enough for him in meeting his goals, he may well decide to use the potential he knows he has to succeed in the educational system.

WORK: DOES IT BUILD CHARACTER?

The idea has a certain appeal: put students to work in their spare time so they'll become more responsible and have less opportunity to be led astray. In the past, people have been very supportive of this view that part-time employment will build character, and some psychologists have even prescribed work as an antidote for adolescent rebellion. The hope was that placing teenagers in jobs where they would have to take on adult responsibilities would displace any thoughts of challenging authority that might have been lurking in their minds. Sounds great and, believe me, if employment were proven to make young people more compliant, I'd be donating members of our household to the work force tomorrow. But, as usual, things aren't that simple.

The issue of student employment is particularly relevant for parents in North America. The number of teenagers working while attending full-time education has risen steadily. For example, in 1940 fewer than 5 percent had a part-time job. During the last two decades, however, surveys have indicated that 80 percent will be employed at some point during their high school years. At any one time, approximately half of students in the 16 to 19 age range are employed; this rises to 75 percent among older students.

Not only is the incidence of employment much greater, students are also working longer hours. In one study it was found that over half of the senior students who had jobs were working more than 20 hours a week. The trend is clear: students have become an important part of the national workforce. Their presence has increased in many sectors, most notably retail and wholesale trade and accommodation and food services.

How much character-building actually goes on? Like many parents, we'd hoped our oldest child would mature when she got her first part-time job. In a way she did. Joanne's supervisor at the local library was very pleased with her. She was always on time, and I remember how stunned we were to see her up and presentable at eight o'clock on a Saturday morning. And later when she was working in a doughnut store, we learned how readily she followed instructions and took the initiative to see that her work was completed as expected. After a while our pleasure and disbelief turned to mild resentment. We realized she was definitely growing up, but not for us. If she'd adopted the same approach to her job as she usually did to her household chores, customers would have been eating day-olds by the time they were served or, during a particularly bad stretch, would have been in danger of wearing their Boston creams.

We weren't alone in finding the work habits and attitudes demonstrated on the job didn't extend to other areas. When groups of students have been studied, the results have failed to show a higher level of responsibility among those who work. Perhaps it's simply a question of choice. If you want to keep a job, you either know, or learn very quickly, that you really have no option when it comes to following instructions. "I'll do it later" or "Why should I?" don't get you very far with employers. At home, however, such lines can be a standard introduction to the type of debate and conflict most families experience at some time or another.

Another argument for part-time employment is that it helps students acquire work-related skills. To some extent this may be true, but only in a very limited sense. Having the responsibility of a job may help young people learn to organize their time more effectively. Most of the jobs held, however, involve largely repetitive and manual activities, like stacking books on library shelves and serving fast food—skills that won't typically be of much help in pursuing the kinds of career goals many students set for themselves.

But if they work, you may think they'll be saving for their education or, better still, so they can look after you in your golden years. Saving accounts may be opened, but for the most part these are no more than temporary holding places. It's your local retail and entertainment industries that are reaping the benefits; some 80 percent of students spend all or nearly all of their earnings indulging their short-term goals and whims. They buy stereos and clothes, go to movies, and eat lots of fast food. I can still recall how enjoyable it was to first have this type of financial freedom and power, and I don't begrudge others this pleasure. But it remains the case that most adolescents don't handle money in ways that would objectively be more sensible, such as setting aside a portion as an investment for their future.

At this time I should state that I won't be trying to convince you that teenagers shouldn't mix school and work; this is a matter that needs to be decided on an individual basis, taking into account factors such as the number of hours to be worked and the young person's academic abilities. Problems can develop if the student is working relatively long hours; the danger zone seems to begin as they approach 20 hours a week. Grades tend to decrease, and the student is likely to pick courses that are less demanding and potentially of less value to them. Furthermore, the likelihood of truancy and leaving school before graduating increases significantly. Not unexpectedly, it's the marginal students who are at greatest risk. If they are already struggling with their courses and putting in a 20-hour workweek, it's no surprise their grades begin to suffer.

Alcohol and drug abuse are also higher among students who work long hours. Why this is so is unclear, but premature affluence and the more ready access to alcohol and drugs this brings could be factors. It may also be that the stress and boredom often associated with long hours of routine, menial work increase the likelihood that teenagers will look to drinking or drugs for excitement.

While the research has its limitations, the results to date haven't confirmed the belief that part-time employment necessarily has beneficial effects for students. This doesn't mean that teenagers shouldn't work. If right now your daughter or son is out of the house slinging burgers or pumping gas, I recommend you do no more than enjoy the peace and quiet. The only caution would be that parents and teenagers need to be aware of how important it can be to balance work and school. Provided the hours of employment aren't too high, I wouldn't be concerned about the possibility that part-time work would expose them to unnecessary risks. This may be particularly true for younger teens; parents of ninth-graders seem to generally approve of their daughter's or son's employment. As students get older, the need to balance school and work may become more critical, as senior high school students face tougher academic demands and tend to work longer hours. Parents can find themselves worried about the degree of independence that has been obtained, conflicts regarding use of money and leisure time can arise, and signs that school performance is slipping may develop.

When our children reached adolescence we encouraged them to have at least some involvement in the working world. But this intention is no more than a matter of personal preference. Our expectation has been that they'll assume some of the responsibility for funding their lifestyles. At the same time, we know a family in which the parents have a very different point of view. Their three sons haven't been allowed to work at all during high school, and in keeping with what we know from the research, they're far from showing any signs of being irresponsible or overly dependent.

THE DOMESTIC LABOR FORCE

In modern-day households where there's too much work to go around and rarely a full-time homemaker, it's entirely reasonable to expect the children to pitch in. The rush to prepare meals is a common beginning to the "second shift" for families where there's no stay-at-home parent. Younger children can assist, and once their apprenticeship is complete, can take a turn preparing the family meal. Although I'm not willing to admit it to his face, Aaron, by the age of 17, had fine-tuned his skills to the point where his pasta sauce was better than mine. After many years of kitchen duty, it was such a pleasure to have a meal cooked for us. It also reaffirmed our belief that there's justice in the world; however petty this may seem, we chuckled quietly when Aaron became irate because the rest of us didn't hurry to the table after he called us for supper.

You should go into the labor recruitment drive with your eyes open. Be prepared for resistance. Don't expect to hear, "Thank you for giving me the opportunity to contribute to the household and, in some small way, repay you for everything you do for me. I think I'll skip going out with my friends today and get right to my jobs." Resistance can take the form of feigned incompetence. Most of us are familiar with this strategy, although we'd probably deny it under cross-examination. I have no interest in disproving Kathy's view that I'm incapable of doing the laundry without shrinking the most expensive item of clothing in the pile; for her part, Kathy shows no sign of mounting a coup to oust me from my position as cook. So don't be surprised if your otherwise bright, resourceful, and self-confident teen acts as if the intricacies of pushing a broom are beyond him.

Resistance can also take the form of "it's not fair." Older siblings can complain they have more to do than younger ones. Assignment of tasks and expectations, however, should be based on age and development. This guiding principle is used outside the family as well; the student in grade three doesn't have as much homework as one in grade 12. At home, he goes to bed earlier and doesn't get to use the car; but neither does he have to mow the lawn or do the laundry. When he gets older, he too will have the responsibilities and privileges that come with age. He can also expect to inherit the chores left behind when his sibling moves out.

In addition to fostering independence, involvement in running the house has a positive impact on children's social development. This effect has been noted by Joan Grusee and her associates at the University of Toronto. Adolescents who were assigned work that benefited the whole family were rated relatively high on a measure of the concern they had for other people. What may seem like a chore can, in effect, be one of those valuable learning experiences that children need. It really is for their own good, as well as reducing the stress on their working parents.

It can sound like a huge leap to connect division of the family workload to bonding and attachment, but let me give it a try. I have a preference for shared labor at home. There will, of course, be times when children have sole responsibility for a chore and will be expected to display independence. But there can also be opportunities to work together. Last weekend, Aaron and I worked together cleaning up the backyard. He played his music and I kept my comments to myself. His silent suffering was interspersed with conversation and his rate of finding excuses to take a break was far less than when he's out there on his own. The job was finished with a minimum of fuss, and he was good company to boot.

The term "togetherness" doesn't typically conjure up images of conjoint dishwashing, laundry folding, and bathroom cleaning, but I suggest at least entertaining this expanded definition. Being together doesn't have to apply only to recreational and other enjoyable activities; many parents want more time with their children, and redistributing the workload can help accomplish this goal, while simultaneously reducing the demands on the overworked family members.

GENDER BOUNDARIES REVISITED

One of the pressing issues when Kiera was 15 was whether or not she'd be expected to operate the lawn mower and snow blower when she became the senior child-in-residence. Aaron was finishing high school and would be leaving home in the fall. The lawn mower issue was being hotly debated. Kiera, who by no means has been brought up in a traditional family, showed no hesitation or compunction when asserting that operating such machines was a "boy's job." I was getting worried. If she prevailed in instating stereotypical gender roles, I'd have to face the fact that I was the only male left. We compromised.

It's common for gender bias to be evident in assignment of household chores, even in families where the parents genuinely hold egalitarian attitudes. As might be predicted, cutting the grass, small repairs, and washing the car are often designated as "male" tasks and given to fathers and sons. "Female" tasks such as cleaning and cooking are more likely to be carried out by a mother or daughter.

Ignoring traditional gender boundaries during the recruitment drive has two advantages. The first is that no one can get away with using their gender to claim they're not qualified for the job. The second is that it helps create an atmosphere of gender equality, with all of its attendant benefits. In retrospect, I should have applied this line of reasoning with Kiera, although I doubt she'd have been convinced that each time she started the lawn mower she was striking a blow for feminism.

PLAY

The idea that we over-organize and "program" our children was the subject of an article in *Time*. In "The Quest for a Superkid," authors Jeffrey Kluger and Alice Park talked of children filling what few spare hours they have with a "buffet line of outside activities that may or may not build character but definitely build résumés. Kids who once had childhoods now have curriculums." This sentiment is not new; concern about the tendency to force too much learning on children led one 19th-century writer to warn about the dangers of attempting to "develop the flower before the stalk is grown." David Elkind introduced the same theme when he began writing about the "hurried child" in the early 1980s; he later published a book with the same title. He deplored the "increasing and unrelenting stress on today's young people" and was critical of parents for burdening their children with excessive and unrealistic expectations.

The notion of the hurried child has been supported in the social science research. Susan Shaw at the University of Waterloo, for example, undertook a survey of high school students in Ontario. She found that "time stress" was common. Close to half of the students felt rushed in their day-to-day lives, with the stress coming from both school and extracurricular activities. She also found this stress was more common among girls than boys.

One fanciful solution was proposed by a panel member during a radio discussion of adolescent stress. He was all set to make a pile of money. He planned to build a chain of summer camps—Camp Hang-Around. It would be a low-budget operation as there would be absolutely no programming. Forget sailing, water skiing, canoeing, and wilderness treks. His only major investment would be a mock-up of a street corner and converting a barn to resemble a shopping mall. He'd charge parents large sums of money to ensure they felt they were paying for a high quality experience and the kids would just "veg" for the summer.

For the most part, the modern generation of teenagers experiences the same high level of demands on their time as their parents, and it's important for them to develop their recreational lives. The choices they make at this stage in their lives will also set the pattern for adulthood. For example, over 1,500 high school students who had taken part in a study of leisure activities were reassessed when they were in their fifties. Those who had been heavily involved in sports, artistic activities, intellectual pursuits, or formal organizations tended to maintain this involvement into middle age.

Leisure activities not only reduce stress but also keep teens occupied. The saying, "the devil finds work for idle hands" has received empirical support. Young people who are involved in recreational activities are less likely to display major problems such as delinquency. Recreation also has a positive impact on self-esteem and social development. One study tracked over 10,000 students and looked at the impact of extracurricular activities at school. Students who signed up for such activities tended to score higher on measures of social and academic self-esteem. On average, they also spent more time on their homework and obtained higher marks. The overall pattern of results suggested that extracurricular pursuits added to the students' commitment to all aspects of school.

A recent study published in the *International Journal of Drug Policy* surveyed the reasons given by preteens and teens for their decisions about whether or not to begin using illegal drugs. Reasons for saying no included the concern that drugs would interfere with other activities and pursuits they valued and enjoyed. Among those who used drugs, boredom and the wish to have more enjoyment in their lives emerged as the major reasons. Other studies have also established a link between boredom and inactivity and both alcohol abuse and delinquency.

Involvement in leisure and recreational activities is, of course, only one of many factors contributing to substance abuse and delinquency; the sight of your daughter moping around the house complaining of new heights of boredom isn't a sure-fire sign of imminent moral decay. Parents can be reassured, however, that the time, money, and occasional cajoling needed to involve their children in recreational and leisure pursuits is a worthwhile investment.

As yet, we don't know very much about the extent to which a particular type of leisure activity has a positive influence on other areas of life. Rest assured that the research is on its way. I particularly like the article "Juvenile Jazz Bands and the Moral Universe of Healthy Leisure Time." The title guaranteed I'd read on. The author talked about the positive influence of becoming involved in an organization such as a band; he claimed, for example, that it fosters self-discipline and even patriotism. Get them signed up! But my all-time favorite is entitled "Common Leisure Activities of Pets and Children." Adolescents who own pets (at least those in Germany, where the study was conducted) read more than those who don't. My first inclination was to advertise this research and buy a pet store. Then I continued reading. Pet owners are also more likely to visit discos. "Why?" you may ask. Like you, I'll have to wait for the next instalment to find out, but I share the concern I'm sure you now have regarding the likely fate of those innocent gerbils, mutts, and goldfish whose owners had upset their parents by frequenting the local discotheques.

It doesn't follow that all socially acceptable forms of recreation should be encouraged. Watching television has been cited as an example of a popular activity that may have a negative impact on teens. It's somewhat alarming that watching television emerges as the second most time-consuming activity for young people; the first is sleeping. By the time most students graduate from high school they've typically spent more time in front of the television than they have in the classroom.

As I'm writing, I can hear the sounds of my wife's car being cleaned. The same son who has such an affinity for couches and channel changers is responsible. This isn't, however, an act of kindness on his part. He's been treated to one of his mother's motivational speeches; this particular one lists the unspeakable consequences he'll face if doesn't get off his backside and do something that at least gives his heart a reason to beat. The research supports her refusal to feel any pangs of guilt at her failure to negotiate such matters.

Watching television is a passive process in two ways. The first is obvious; it's about as far removed from aerobic activity as is possible when you're awake. It's not surprising that teenagers who watch many hours of television a day are less likely to be fit and are at greater risk for obesity. The second effect is less direct. Although adolescents may watch television and movies in the company of others, the level of social involvement is minimal. As passive members of the audience, they have little need or desire to interact, and there is, therefore, no opportunity to develop their social skills.

Video games came under the spotlight after the tragic shootings in high schools in Canada and the United States. There were media reports of how much time the teenage assailants had spent playing violent video games. Subsequent studies also heightened awareness of how frequently violence is the main theme in video games; one study reported that 90 percent of video games aimed at the teenager and adult audiences have violent content. Calls to ban or restrict their availability followed.

The possibility that playing violent video games leads to violent behavior is obviously an important question to ask, but it's an extremely difficult one to answer. Cause and effect are notoriously hard to establish for such issues. There are several studies demonstrating that young people who spend a great deal of their time playing violent games are more likely than average to exhibit aggressive behavior. But this doesn't necessarily mean that playing the violent games *causes* real life aggression. Other explanations are plausible. For example, it could be that young people who are already aggressive choose to play violent video games. If this is true, playing these games is the result of being aggressive in the first place—it doesn't cause violence. The argument has also been made that adolescents could play violent video games because they provide a safe outlet for aggression. As one theorist speculated, perhaps the violent game offers "a safe, private laboratory where they can experience different emotions, including those that are controversial in ordinary life."

Experiments have been designed to address the question of cause and effect. Teenagers have been randomly assigned to groups: one plays a violent video game, while the other plays a nonviolent game. A variety of measures are used to see if the groups differ in their subsequent levels of aggression. Significant effects have been reported—for example, with respect to the amount of empathy or hostility conveyed when asked to evaluate stories depicting interpersonal conflict. One study even used brain imaging to determine that violent video games had an impact on the activity in one of the areas responsible for regulation of emotion. It can be difficult, however, to determine how far results from laboratory studies can be generalized to everyday situations: the measures used often seem far removed from real-life violence, particularly extreme forms such as the high school shootings.

Although more research is needed, the studies to date demonstrate that video game violence can have at least some influence on aggression. Moreover, there seems to be no support for the view that it might have beneficial effects. When parents raise this issue with me, I suggest moderation and monitoring. The amount of time and the degree of violence fall under the former. Playing video games can consume too much of a young person's time and energy, and articles about video game addiction have been appearing. Moderation in content is also called for. Most parents wouldn't want their sons playing a video game where they can pick up prostitutes, have sex, and kill them for their money. Such games have been bestsellers.

Having set up a few guidelines, parents can quietly monitor the situation. If signs of excessive preoccupation with video games appear or changes in behavior become evident, more restrictions or a complete ban may be necessary. Otherwise, there's probably no reason to be concerned. Millions of teens play video games that contain violence without becoming violent themselves, just as they emerge unscarred from watching violent movies and playing "army" or "cops and robbers" when they're younger.

I tend to believe there's nothing inherently "bad" about activities such as watching television and playing video games. At times it seems the potential benefits of both are ignored. Television programs can be informative and they can address important teenage issues in a balanced way. Video games can also challenge the mind; they can require both problem-solving skills and creativity. We need to be sure, however, that neither activity interferes with important aspects of adolescent development. Aaron has resumed his position on the couch and the channel changer is in high gear. But he shouldn't make himself too comfortable. He can be assured that his mother is working on yet another of her motivational speeches.

Although we don't know a great deal about the effects of particular leisure activities, they can provide a way for young people to increase their range of involvement with peers and the community in general. The need for adolescents to begin separating from the family and establishing their own identity will be discussed in Chapter 13, and developing recreational interests is undoubtedly an important part of this process.

CHAPTER 10

LIFESTYLE

"When I was your age" isn't an introduction that resonates with teenagers. Understandably, not many have an insatiable appetite for tales of our youth. But for those of us who like to reminisce, there's virtue to remembering bygone days. From the age of five we walked just under a mile each way to and from school—probably more when the detours and meandering are taken into account. We organized our own activities in the evenings and on weekends, which typically involved a lot of walking and running. We were rarely chauffeured and preferred to spend our allowance on essentials such as candy and comic books rather than bus fare. Studies tell us the food portions served at home were smaller in those days than they are now. There was less processed food and less fast food.

Our lives were certainly not care-free, but if we'd ever thought about such matters, I'm sure we'd have predicted the world's future was secure. No one talked about global warming, greenhouse gases, or the ozone layer, and there were no credible predictions that life on planet Earth, as we knew it, could come to an end within a century.

In these respects, things aren't what they used to be. In their paper "Costs and Consequences of Sedentary Living," Frank Booth and Manu Chakravarthy coined the term "sedentary death syndrome" to express the concern that today's children may not outlive their parents. Similarly, obesity is frequently referred to as an "epidemic" that poses a serious threat to their health. I was reviewing a *Degrassi Talks* video in which high school students were interviewed about the issues in their lives that made them unhappy. One teen in Alberta commented, "This may be the hardest time for kids to have to grow up in." He wondered if he was contributing to the destruction of the environment and was already worrying about the legacy he'd be leaving his children.

One of the challenges for parents has become teaching their children how to develop and maintain a lifestyle that will keep them and their environment healthy. I remain optimistic: there are many things we can do that allow us to meet this challenge.

EXERCISE

My wife can't believe I have the nerve to write about exercise. She pointed out that credible authors have usually had at least some experience in the field. I can't deny that I come from a long line of slugs. My brother and I were always pleased when we were picked last for teams; it reassured us that our teammates' expectations of what we'd contribute were realistic. We were made to play rugby at school. The coach assumed that because I was tall for my age I was athletic; he soon learned the truth. He'd berate me for not pursuing the ball, but I simply didn't want it. I knew how to share—if that mean-looking fellow on the other team wanted it so badly, he was welcome to it. The pinnacle of my school athletic career was placing second in an egg-and-spoon race at the age of nine.

To salvage any credibility I might have had before you started reading this section, let me argue that my history makes me especially qualified to talk about the importance of exercise for teens. If your daughter or son is already a card-carrying jock who doesn't realize that a "good sweat" is an oxymoron, you can skip this part of the book. They need no help in this area; in fact, chances are good that their interest in athletic and other physical pursuits will be life-long. One factor predicting both later fitness and more general adjustment is childhood involvement in a broad range of extracurricular activities such as sports. For the rest of us who "hit the wall" while we're still doing up our running shoes, a different approach is needed. Here is where I can strive to be a role model; I have an instant connection with the couch potatoes of the world, and changing this aspect of my lifestyle hasn't been easy, but it has met with modest success.

The first question is this: does exercise really add to the quality of life or is this proposition part of a huge plot driven by the greed of international sportswear conglomerates? I regret to say there's no evidence to support the latter view. There is, however, an abundance of evidence proving that exercise does improve the quality of our lives. There's also no doubt that people of all ages need to increase their level of physical activity. This message has been delivered by educators and health care specialists for many years, yet the statistics tell us nearly half of North American youth are still not active on a regular basis. What's worse, the trend over the past decade has been a decline in overall physical activity. One factor may be that many of the benefits aren't obvious but have to do with prevention. To a generally healthy teenager, exercising to avoid the risk of Type 2 diabetes, hypertension, osteoporosis, and heart disease in later life is unlikely to be seen as a priority.

Differences in values and priorities also play a role. Studies with teens show that achievement—as defined by academic success—is a major goal for some, while fitness and health is the priority for others. Both areas are, of course, important and there's no reason why they can't coexist as goals. The implication, however, is that you may have a son or daughter who, like the author of this book, needs serious help in the exercise department.

Social support is once again important. Friends become increasingly influential in determining the level of physical activity, just as they do in other domains. By grade seven, companionship and feelings of social competence are among the major benefits of participating in activities such as sports. But the studies also tell us that parents can have an influence in several simple ways.

- **Provide information about the value of physical activity.** Providing such information may sound unnecessary, but teenagers may not, in fact, be aware of the short- and long-term benefits. They're likely to be motivated by the social benefits—worrying about heart disease or osteoporosis comes later. Lectures on the topic may not be greeted with enthusiasm, but the occasional comment can reinforce the message that their sports activities aren't just for fun but also keep them healthy. More immediate incentives can be more energy, sleeping more soundly, better control of appetite and weight, more efficient study skills, and lower mental stress.

- **Suggest activities that teens will feel are within their current range of competence.** One factor predicting whether or not adolescents will become involved in physical pursuits is the extent to which they believe they have the potential to succeed. I can relate to this. I did sign up for—and this time complete a yoga class. I didn't go near the center, however, before I had an iron-clad guarantee that "Beginners Class" was a promise and not just a ploy to import comic relief for the other participants. Suggesting activities that teens will feel are within their range of competence is especially important for those with limited experience in athletics or with obstacles such as obesity.

- **Suggest goals and educate their teens about the benefits of relatively minor increases in physical activity.** The "doing what comes naturally" principle can be of value; build on what your children normally do, or have done in the past, rather than trying to radically change their activities and routines. Walking and cycling are examples.

    Walking, in particular, has earned status as the most available and by far the easiest form of exercise. It involves no expense and doesn't inflict pain. It also requires no training, although books have been written on the topic should you feel the need for a refresher course. (I browsed through one not so long ago; it was bursting with pictures and illustrations about topics such as body posture and arm position. No doubt there will be a sequel finally revealing the secret of that age-old dilemma—how to walk and chew gum at the same time.) The main point is that walking is a normal part of our lives.

- **Emphasize small changes.** The belief that fitness means going from couch potato to jock makes the task overwhelming and totally unrealistic. Increasing daily physical activity by only five minutes a week makes it manageable. In just six weeks the goal of an extra half hour each day can be reached, which can lead to a major improvement in fitness.

    One way to illustrate that every little bit helps is to look at a METs chart, which is easily found on the Internet. A MET is a metabolic equivalent, and 1 MET is the rate of energy expended when sitting quietly. Playing the piano or washing dishes get you to 2.3 and walking briskly tops 3. Fishing can also hit 3 provided you're awake and casting the odd time. If you dig your own worms with a shovel you're at 4 (it really is in the chart). Someone also felt the need to measure how much energy it takes to jingle dance—the score came in at 5.5. The list is long and can assist in selecting activities that are both enjoyable and realistic, as well as progressively more energetic. As you might expect, running and sports such as rugby fall at the upper end, requiring ten to 20 times the energy needed for loafing around, depending on how much the participants push themselves.

- **Cheer them on whenever possible.** Although all of our children reached the stage when they wanted to deny they even had parents, let alone be seen in public with them, they never objected to our coming to their basketball games, rugby tournaments, or dance recitals. In fact, only a few days ago Alexandra thanked me for driving over an hour to watch her rugby game. I'm not expecting this to be followed by an invitation to hang out with her on the weekend; I'm content just to know that my support and interest meant something to her.

- **Be a good parental model.** The next item puts me to shame— parental modeling. Fortunately Kathy has set the example in the family; this is one area in which I don't mind being ignored by our children. As reviewed by Susan Duncan and her colleagues at the Oregon Research Institute, modeling can be direct or indirect. The direct form involves sharing the activity with your son or daughter. Indirect modeling occurs when teens live in an environment in which exercise and sports are part of their parents' way of life. Modeling is one of the known predictors of how active children will be in their adolescent years.

- **Make it known that, as far as possible, you'll provide instrumental support such as funding certain activities and being available for transportation.**

- **Encourage siblings to be more supportive.** Much depends, of course, on the sibling relationship. Had I been into sports, I know my brother would have shown interest in watching only if the event pitted me against a gladiator with attitude or a ravenous lion. But if there's a sibling who is so inclined, encourage them to be a spectator or support their sister or brother in some other way.

- **Take account of individual preferences and personalities.** Some young people thrive on competition, and sports teams may be a good choice for them. Others have a definite aversion to highly competitive pursuits and may be far more motivated for cooperative or solitary activities such hiking, fitness classes, and biking.

- **Increase opportunities to be physically active.** One example is a variant of the "take the stairs instead of the elevator" maxim. Suggest changes in transportation, such as driving them only partway to school or a friend's house. Plan family outings that involve physical activities. Going to a place where you can play frisbee guarantees a MET of at least 3, and if you can swim, the energy expenditure is more than doubled. If they're enthusiastic shoppers, plan to go to the entrance farthest away from the stores they intend to visit. The advent of super malls has meant that going from one end to the other is quite a jaunt. Believe it or not, articles have been written on the merits of "mall walking."

- **Consider having exercise tapes and basic equipment available at home.** Several researchers have found that home-based exercising is particularly effective for certain people. For example, teens who are very self-conscious about their abilities or weight may prefer to exercise in the privacy of their homes, at least initially.

NUTRITION

In the 40-odd years I knew my Aunt Margaret, she was always on her diet. After 20 years or so, you'd think she'd realize it wasn't working very well, but Aunt Margaret was no quitter. One of her favorite expressions was, "I think it's time for a little something." This was often followed by a line from an old song, bemoaning the fact that so much of what we enjoy isn't good for us: "It's illegal, it's immoral, or it makes you fat."

I'm with my aunt on this issue. I find self-discipline in this area to be nothing short of torture. I'd love to start each day with a pot of coffee and a cinnamon bun. I don't care what you add to it, how you dress it up, or how strong the data happen to be regarding its benefits, bran is bran, and the prospect of eating it first thing in the morning does nothing to brighten my day. But, the truth must be faced, our nutritional habits, and those of our children, are in a sorry state. As discussed in their book *Super Sized Kids*, Dr. Walt Larimore and Sherri Flynt remind us that, as a population, we're "overfed and undernourished." They add, "We may talk healthy, but we eat tasty."

One major consequence of poor nutrition is that more and more young people are overweight, as are their parents. The problem is progressive and often starts early. Inevitably, the results from surveys vary—for example, denial and wishful thinking are probably the reason why estimates of the problem are lower when people report their weight, as opposed to being weighed. Certain conclusions can nonetheless be reached with confidence. There's no doubt that a large number of children and adolescents in North America are overweight or obese. Furthermore, the percentage of young people who are overweight has been increasing. This holds true for both genders and is also particularly evident for teens. A Canadian study, for example, reported an increase from 14 to 29 percent in the 12 to 17 age group since the 1970s. A final comment on the research is perhaps the most important: being overweight tends to be a long-term problem. This finding doesn't mean that change is impossible, but it does speak to the need to address the problem rather than assume or hope the adolescent "puppy fat" will disappear with maturity.

It would be beyond the scope of my profession to tackle issues related to nutrition in any depth. Psychologists have, however, been among those interested in studying eating habits, and I'll review some of the findings that can help parents decide how to improve nutritional habits in the family.

- **Model good eating habits.** The booklet for the *Eat Well Play Hard* program developed by the New York state Department of Health has a cartoon that says it all. Father and son, who are both overweight, are eating chips while watching television. Dad comments, "Get some exercise, Billy, change the channel." There's a strong correlation between teenagers' eating habits and those of their parents. This means, of course, that they can blame us for their bad habits. On the positive side, it also means we can take the lead by modeling a better way of eating if we also need to smarten up. Changing aspects of lifestyle can be a family project in which all members challenge and support one another. It can sometimes be very reassuring for teens to realize their parents also have to struggle when it comes to changing habits that, while unhealthy, have been thoroughly enjoyable.

One starting point is to implement the latest food guide. Adherence in North America is poor; the majority of young people fail to eat the recommended number of servings from each food group. The 40 percent or so who do manage to eat fruits and vegetables five or more times a day not only increase the overall quality of nutrition but also reduce their chances of becoming overweight.

- **Make the first meal of the day the most important.** Having been brought up in Britain, I know the importance of a "hearty breakfast." As I look back on it, the Brits had it half right; skipping breakfast is definitely not a good idea. The half we flunked had to do with content. My favorite start to the day was fried eggs, fried bacon, fried sausage, fried mushrooms, fried tomatoes, and bread (fried, of course, in bacon fat). Nobody measured cholesterol back then and it's a wonder we survived.

  Our knowledge has increased, but that doesn't necessarily mean we're smarter. The majority of six- to 10-year-olds may eat breakfast, but the majority of teenagers don't. Adolescents tend to view eating breakfast with the same enthusiasm they have for cleaning their rooms; less than 50 percent will eat breakfast regularly. The number is especially low for teenage girls who are particularly likely to view their lack of appetite in the morning as a golden opportunity to keep their caloric intake low and avoid weight gain. While this may seem logical, the first meal of the day remains the most important, and for many good reasons. Eating breakfast really does make you smarter—at least temporarily. Going without it makes it harder for nine-year-olds to perform well on tests of memory or visual reasoning, and a bowl of cereal helps students maintain concentration over the course of the morning. Attendance and punctuality also improve, as does overall academic performance.

  As for content, a plate of fried food is rare, and breakfast choices are probably better than they used to be. Those parents wanting to fine-tune the breakfast menu might like to know that, while ready-to-eat cereal has beneficial effects on performance, instant oatmeal appears to give an added boost to the brain cells. The researchers speculated that one difference could be that oatmeal's composition meant it was digested more slowly and, therefore, provided a more sustained energy source—a sort of "slow-release porridge."

- **Give teens the information needed to make good decisions.** Being well-informed may not guarantee that people will make the best decisions, but at least it provides a good starting point. Keeping up with the research in the field of nutrition, however, is far from easy. Butter used to be good for you. It then acquired the status of a banned substance, leaving margarine to corner the market. In moderation, butter is back in favor—at least for now. Eggs went through similar phases. What's the correct balance between protein, carbohydrates, and fats, and which foods have the good, as opposed to the bad cholesterol? Is it really not a good idea to eat after eight at night and which meal should be the biggest?

  Studies abound, and although the findings can be contradictory at times, I assume our knowledge will gradually increase. I cling to the hope that science will soon discover the healing powers of the hot fudge sundae. I've also found the results from a select few studies most reassuring. The recent report that a daily dose of dark chocolate reduces the risk of cardiovascular disease made my day and sent me post-haste to the mall to stock up on my new medicine. Even better, the study involved only men, which justified hiding my stash from my wife.

  Knowledge about nutrition does help teenagers make good decisions, although it's important to be realistic. Knowing what's good for us by no means guarantees that we'll act accordingly, but it's a start. As might be expected, older children tend to have a greater understanding of topics such as food groups and nutritional balance. One study found that greater knowledge of the fat and fiber content of foods led to teenagers making healthier choices.

- **Encourage your teen to make better choices when eating out.** I can still recall the thrill of our annual trip into London to buy shoes when I was a child. Not that my brother and I were particularly concerned about our footwear—it was the promise of a visit to the cafeteria at Marks and Spencers afterward to have lunch. With the exception of vacation trips, this was the only day in the year when we ate out. Apart from the fish and chip shop, "fast food" had yet to be invented in Britain. Over the course of the following decades, availability and use of fast food climbed steadily. Eating out is routine for many young people today. The lunch break at many high schools is marked by a rapid exodus to the nearby pizza and burger joints, and parents line up at the drive-through to make sure their children eat something in the period between finishing school and arriving for their swimming lessons.

  The trend is clear. Adolescents are getting less of their energy intake from eating at home than was the case 10 years ago. With this trend goes a shift in what's consumed—for example, more salty snacks, French fries, and soft drinks, and less nutrient-rich foods such as vegetables, fruit, and milk. The average intake of soft drinks, for example, has sky-rocketed over the past two decades. One survey found that it more than doubled in a period of only four years in the 1990s.

  Quantity has changed as well as quality. The term "supersizing" was made popular in the movie *Super Size Me*. Morgan Spurlock not only made the film, he also ate nothing but fast food for a month, emerging much the worse for the experience. Samara Nielsen and Barrie Popkin of the Department of Nutrition at the University of North Carolina set out to determine just how prevalent supersizing has become. In their 2003 study they compared portion sizes over a 20-year period. They focused on specific foods, including many that would top the popularity chart for teens: chips, hamburgers, French fries, pizza, burritos, tacos, ice cream, cookies, and soft drinks. Portion sizes were measured in different locations: home, fast food restaurants, and other restaurants. With the exception of pizza, all portion sizes increased significantly; this was particularly the case for fast food. The authors referred to the increase as "substantial." Their calculation of the added calories over the course of a year provides convincing evidence that the larger portions would be translated into more pounds.

In principle, eating out isn't the problem, but persuading your son to order carrot sticks rather than fries and go for fresh fruit over a donut may not be easy. Increasing their understanding of nutrition and parental modeling are again important, as is patronizing those fast food restaurants that accomodate healthier choices.

- **Encourage grazing.** Teenagers aren't known for their enthusiasm for helping around the house. In fact, we've coined the term "chores" for those few tasks we ask them to perform. The Webster dictionary defines a chore as a task that is "difficult or disagreeable." Both adjectives would apply to many teenagers when they're asked to do one. Encouraging healthy nutrition can capitalize on this aversion to domesticity. The basic premise is that teenagers are most likely to eat what's readily available and, therefore, requires the least effort on their part. While family meals are important, adolescents are particularly prone to being hungry at other times in the day. This provides a wonderful opportunity to encourage grazing. A platter of cut-up vegetables and fruit may not be requested, but if it appears in a conspicuous spot it may well be devoured.

- **Suggest and support initiatives at school that include physical fitness.** One example is the 5-2-1-Almost None program that has been implemented for high school students. The primary objective is overweight prevention, and it incorporates four goals for each day—namely, 5 servings of fruit and vegetables, no more than 2 hours of screen time, 1 hour or more of physical activity, and almost no sugar-sweetened beverages.

ENVIRONMENT

Last night we had one of our regular get-togethers with three couples—all long-time friends. We livened up the conversation by debating the merits or otherwise of our voting choices at the last federal election. We have a lot in common, but when it comes to politics we cover almost all the bases, which makes for lively conversation. Usually consensus isn't even a remote possibility, but we found ourselves in complete agreement after the topic of the environment was raised. Like many of our generation, we've come to realize that our lifestyles over the past few decades have been a major contributor to many of problems we face, such as climate change and air pollution.

Young people are also becoming increasingly aware of environmental issues and, for some, this has added another source of stress when they think about their future lives. Girls are particularly prone to worrying about the environment. They tend to be more altruistic than boys at this age and, therefore, more concerned about matters that affect the general well-being of the population.

The degree to which young people are confident that solutions will be found is another factor. One study found that anxiety about the environment was most likely to undermine adolescents' sense of well-being when they believed there was little scientists or interest groups could do to save the planet.

I'm not an expert on environmental issues. What I can attempt to do, however, is apply some of the research relating to attitude formation and behavior change to the task of helping young people recognize they can take significant steps to address their growing concern about the world they live in. Adolescents often feel they have little power to effect change; what they can control, however, is their day-to-day behavior. The critical step is realizing they can establish a lifestyle that will protect and heal their environment. There's much parents can do to help teenagers develop the belief they can bring about change. Given the possibility that without lifestyle changes, they—or their children—will be struggling to survive on a planet that has become hostile and uninhabitable, it's hard to think of a more important responsibility facing today's parents.

Social psychologists have studied attitudes and values and their impact on behavior for many decades. As we all know, having a particular value doesn't guarantee that we'll act on it; as my mother said pointedly to me on many occasions during my youth, "The path to hell is paved with good intentions." Nonetheless, developing the appropriate values or attitudes is a good start. Jana Meinhold at Portland State University studied the relationship between pro-environmental attitudes and pro-environmental behavior. Quite clearly, those adolescents who had formed attitudes reflecting environmental concern were the most likely to act accordingly.

Parents are a major source of their children's core values. Ongoing discussion about important matters is one of the main ways we exert this influence. It can be hard, however, to determine exactly what to tell our children about an issue that has the potential to be alarming. One problem is that, while there's very little dispute that the planet is in urgent need of repair, there's hardly any agreement as to how serious the situation has become.

My fallback position is based on the research that the level of anxiety evoked influences the likelihood of attitude change. Using television ads to increase compliance with seat belt legislation serves as an example. When the message is neutral and matter-of-fact, it tends to have little effect. As discussed in Chapter Two, scare tactics are also not recommended; attitudes won't shift if the message uses horrific images that viewers find upsetting. Their response is to shut out the information. But a mid-range level of anxiety does the trick.

People keep watching and they keep listening, and the probability they'll favor use of seat belts and actually use them also increases.

The same mid-ground can be sought for environmental concerns. I want my children to be concerned and I want them to hold the belief that environmental issues are a priority and require action now. I don't, however, want them to feel they're doomed. Al Gore's movie, *An Inconvenient Truth*, is an example of how a candid portrayal of the dangers can be balanced with a clear message of hope.

Values and attitudes create the motivation to do something; motivation doesn't, of course, guarantee that we know how to do it. This is where the role of knowledge is critical. Doctor Meinhold reported that the impact of attitudes on pro-environmental behavior was greatest when adolescents were well informed. All this may sound obvious once you hear it, but the distinction between knowing there's a problem and knowing how to solve it can seem vast when facing environmental issues. A 15-year-old can feel passionately about climate change, but helpless when it comes to doing anything about it. Knowledge will give her the tools she needs to translate values into action.

One study with adolescents suggested parents need to become better role models in the environmental department. An educational program was successful in helping these students recognize the need to mobilize the population to address climate change, but when interviewed, the same students expressed doubt about their parents' ability to change their behavior.

There are many ways parents can model and teach simple, practical steps to care for the environment. Make a family project of building a compost bin, planting a tree, or installing energy-efficient light bulbs; pay a fine to the family recreation fund every time you neglect to turn off a light, computer, or other electrical device; choose and request less packaging in stores; show your daughter how to program thermostats for hot water and heating systems, and have her experiment with a lower setting; make a point of using less hot water (yes, that means shorter showers); make a chart showing the amount of energy and water the family has used every month and set targets for lower consumption; and demonstrate to teenagers how to make their concerns known to the people who will soon want their vote.

Teenagers can also be encouraged to select high school courses that incorporate environmental issues or participate in environmental programs in their community and schools. British Columbia Hydro has a program that involves students in investigating the energy efficiency in their schools, and a "no waste lunch" campaign has been introduced into schools in Minnesota. The Green Schools program in several American states not only integrates environmental issues into the curriculum but also has students involved in reducing energy consumption in their schools and homes. The anti-idle campaign in Mississauga, Ontario, recruits children to be the "ambassadors" who can educate their parents about the importance of turning the engine off when they wait for them after classes. Don't expect sympathy if it's February and the idea of global warming is furthest from your mind. No excuses—your passenger will be armed with the facts. Did *you* know that if every driver in Canada avoided idling for five minutes every day, the weight of the carbon dioxide no longer pumped into the atmosphere would be equal to the weight of 633 African elephants, which, by the way, are the largest land animals in the world? Should that not convince you, give them a pen and paper, and they can apply the formula from math class to tell you just how much greenhouse gas you pumped into the atmosphere while you were idling away the time waiting for them.

CHAPTER 11

CYBERKIDS

WELCOME TO CYBERSPACE

A recent survey of adolescents included the question: "How has the Internet changed your life?" The otherwise vocal respondents looked puzzled and were stumped for an answer. The researchers soon realized the question made no sense to this generation. The Internet hadn't changed their lives, it had always been part of their lives. While a number of their parents might view cyberspace as a mysterious and daunting environment, it was familiar territory to them.

Most teenagers in North America have access to the Internet at home. Others have access at school, libraries, and friends' houses. Add to this the increasing numbers of cell phones with Internet capability and you have a generation of young people who are enthusiastic inhabitants of cyberspace. Parents, on the other hand, have a love-hate relationship with the Internet. A recent survey conducted by Common Sense Media reported that as much as parents are intrigued by its power and capabilities, they worry about its potential dangers.

Before addressing the concerns about teenagers' use of the Internet, I'd like to extol its two biggest virtues. The first is that it offers the world's largest library. If your daughter were writing an essay on endangered species, the Internet would locate 38,400,000 sites ("hits") that at least make reference to this topic. Fortunately, she doesn't have to sift through them all. Chances are good the first few pages will lead to sites that provide the information she's after. A project on the French Revolution would net only 8,230,000 hits, but it would at least be a start. What's even more impressive is how fast the Internet will respond when asked for information. There's no lining up to speak to the librarian or use the computer catalog system. Those 38 million or so hits for endangered species were located in less than one-fifth of a second. It truly boggles the mind.

The second virtue of the Internet is that it offers a wonderful way of communicating with people. You can "chat" to relatives and friends from all over the world. This communication often involves instant messaging, which occurs in real time. For the uninitiated, all this means is that you're both sitting at the computer and can read what the other person is typing as they type it. Webcams will also allow your son to see his grandparents on the screen while talking to them, even if they live on the other side of the world.

Fire up the computer, and you have the opportunity to communicate with like-minded strangers on any topic imaginable. Assume that you have an all-consuming interest in collecting bottles or urgently need to know how to fillet a catfish. Who can you call? If you don't happen to know anyone with the same interest or need, the Internet is there to serve you. Let me give you an example. If you ever find yourself in Hilton Head, South Carolina, and like seafood, you must go to the Bonefish Grill and have their "bang bang shrimp." It's one of their renowned specialties, and my only complaint is that no amount of begging, pleading, or bribing could persuade the chef to divulge the recipe. A few seconds on the Internet, however, put me in touch with the community of bang bang shrimp lovers, many of whom have experimented with recipes with the same determination shown by the alchemists who tried to make gold—but with much more success. The dish is now part of our cooking repertoire (you're welcome to email me at my website for the recipe).

The number of groups you can visit or join is endless. Some exist primarily to share information. As an example, I just paid a quick visit to one of the many sites devoted to Elvis sightings. Did you know he was sighted a few weeks ago in a supermarket in Northants, England, not long after he asked someone in California for directions to Tennessee? Not such good directions, but it's great to know the King is still with us. Other sites provide the opportunity to meet people—the most common are the "chat rooms." As is the case with many pen pal relationships, you may never have direct contact with the other people in the group, but that doesn't preclude getting to know them and developing a genuine friendship. There are chat rooms for all interests and all ages; some are specifically for teens and children.

By the time girls reach grade six, their most preferred activity on the Internet is chatting with other people, usually their friends. After reaching high school, they spend an average of just over an hour a day socializing on the Internet. In a way the world is much the same as it was a generation ago. Their mothers probably came home after school and spent the next hour with the telephone receiver glued to their ear; it's only the technology that has changed. Boys' number one choice is to play games on the Internet, but they, too, will use it as part of their social lives.

SO WHAT'S ALL THE FUSS ABOUT?

Now for the not so good news. The Internet may be the world's biggest library and a vast communication system, but it operates with very few controls and safeguards. I'll be highlighting aspects of the Internet that are disturbing and shocking. I don't, however, believe it's necessary to ban children from the Internet. Just as parents prepare their children to deal with the dangers of the physical community, they can prepare them to deal with the dangers of cyberspace. The key is knowledge and communication, both of which will be discussed throughout this chapter.

The fact that the Internet gives young people ready access to vast amounts of information is both exciting and concerning. One challenge for them is to learn how to distinguish between valid information and gibberish. If I decided to write a book about the French Revolution I'd be faced with many obstacles. Given my prior confession that I had a major attitude problem when it came to learning history at high school, I'd have little to pass on to the reading public, except to say that many heads were chopped off, much to the delight of the local knitting circle. Should I decide not to let ignorance stand in my way, I might find my agent less than receptive when I pitch the book to him. But with the Internet at my disposal, I don't need him. I can post a website: "All You Ever Wanted to Know About the French Revolution but Were Afraid to Ask Your Teacher." Of course, you still won't have the correct answer after visiting my website, but there's nothing stopping me from filling it with idle speculation or pure fantasy dressed up as fact.

A related problem is how to ensure young people don't obtain material their parents deem inappropriate. You can send your son off to the library secure in the knowledge that the shelves won't be stocked with hard-core pornography or hate literature. Laws and basic library practice will ensure they aren't available. But both are examples of material that's readily found on the Internet. Teens don't have to be looking for this material; I'll give examples of how easily they can be unintentionally exposed to information and images that may upset or confuse them.

Meeting others on the Internet also entails risk, but it's very hard to know where the danger is lurking. Most of the time there's little to worry about. The Internet may attract all sorts of people, but most sorts of people are just fine. After all, we don't typically expect to have negative encounters with the strangers we meet in our day-to-day lives. Asking for directions when we're lost or sitting next to someone on a city bus aren't exactly high-risk behaviors. But, as we all know, there are a few strangers who'd wish us or our children harm and some of them inhabit cyberspace. The Internet offers them an unequaled opportunity to prey on potential victims.

In his classic book *The Presentation of Self in Everyday Life*, sociologist Erving Goffman discusses how we're always selective in the way we present ourselves to other people. There are aspects of ourselves we want to highlight and aspects of ourselves we want to mask. But there are limits to how selective we can be in our direct contact with others. Faking your gender and approximate age are obvious examples. The Internet, however, gives us carte blanche when it comes to self-presentation.

Before discussing the dangers, it's worthwhile noting that most efforts to present a fictitious self-image are quite harmless. A cartoon was circulated recently showing a dog using an Internet dating service. He's on the small and scraggy side and definitely a mongrel. His friends are laughing hysterically as they stand around coaching him: "Tell her you're a guard dog, a Rottweiler, and that you're single and neutered." Most adolescents will, at some point, have created a false identity for themselves on the Internet. Studies tell us they often pretend to be older, as well as more accomplished athletically or academically, than they really are. (As an aside, they also report being most put out on discovering that others on the Internet have lied about themselves, but such outrage doesn't seem to deter them from doing the same.)

Just as I could claim to be Professor Peter Marshall, much-acclaimed history scholar, I could tout myself as a muscle-bound jock (yes, you can even stretch things that far). But I could also pretend to be a 13-year-old girl who wants to meet other girls my age. I could easily find a fitting photograph to accompany my bio, and purchasing a few magazines would bring me up to speed with respect to the music, fashion, books, and movies popular among this age group. Visiting a few chat rooms would also give me a crash course on how to talk like a young teen. Now we're in scary territory.

PORNOGRAPHY ON THE INTERNET

My interest in this topic led me to wonder how much our own children had been exposed to hard-core pornography. Somehow I doubted this had been extensive. When I was their age, you were a hero among your peers if you possessed one or two photographs of nude women and were willing to host a study group at recess. So I decided to raise this topic one Sunday dinner. Present were our three youngest children: two teenage daughters and one of their older brothers, in his early twenties. A lull in the conversation prompted me to casually enquire if they'd been exposed to pornography on the Internet.

Aaron looked at me aghast and suggested that perhaps this wasn't a suitable topic for Sunday dinner conversation. Fortunately, Kathy explained that my interest in this question was academic rather than perverse. One of the girls eventually broke the silence, revealing that she'd seen pornographic pictures when she was eight. She also went on to recall an incident that occurred several years ago while visiting a friend. Both were dancers and were surfing the Internet, delighted to find videos of different types of dancing. One of the videos, however, turned out to be pornographic. I've watched countless dance recitals over the years and can assure you I've never witnessed a performance like the one Alexandra saw that night. Her friend's mother came into the room at that point, leaving the girls to convince her their intentions had been innocent.

One confession led to another. The list included bestiality, group sex, and sexual activity involving defecation. I endeavored to remain calm, but I was truly shocked. Clearly we hadn't provided sufficient education and supervision. One reason was our ignorance; neither Kathy nor I were aware of the type of pornography that was so prevalent on the Internet. I wondered what the impact had been and asked if they felt viewing pornography had affected their view of sex in any way. One of the girls responded that it hadn't, as she knew we wouldn't do anything "weird like that." She had, however, answered my question in a tone suggesting that she wanted to add, "Would you?"

The ensuing silence was uncomfortable, to say the least. I reminded myself that, as a psychologist who had worked extensively in areas related to sexuality, I should be more than capable of handling the situation. So I stood up and asked, "Anyone for dessert?" Several conversations with the children were, however, called for and took place over the ensuing weeks. Although such discussions can be awkward and difficult at times, young people need to know what is healthy and safe sex. Without this knowledge, they're ill-equipped to protect themselves against the type of pornography they'll almost inevitably see by the time they reach adolescence. It's a safe bet this pornography is far removed from any images seen by their parents in their adolescence. It depicts all imaginable forms of sexual behaviour, is particularly degrading to women, and is often violent.

I now give workshops on the topic to parents and provide examples of how easy it is for such exposure to happen, either by design or accidentally. A search for "porn" will net over 490 million hits. Not all by any means will contain pornography itself, but it's guaranteed many listed on the first page will. Accidental exposure is also common. Years ago a parent recalled sitting at the computer with her daughter who was a Spice Girls fan. The objective was to find a fan club site. Nine of the 10 sites on the first page were about the Spice Girls. The last, however, turned out to be a group of spicy girls who had forgotten to get dressed before the camera shoot. A recent personal example of accidental exposure comes to mind. I was surfing the Internet for video clips relating to mother-daughter attachment. The first page of the search advertised a site with access to videos of incest and rape. In retrospect, it isn't hard to see how these searches could have found links to pornography, so let me give you an example that surprised me as much as it did the parent who recalled the incident. She was sitting with her 10-year-old son at the computer helping him with his project on gecko lizards. All was going as planned as they navigated their way through different sites; somehow, one was linked to pornography.

Approximately 25 percent of young people report being dis-tressed by the pornographic material they'd viewed. I suspect this underestimates the impact. As discussed over Sunday dinner, my daughter's reaction had been one of confusion rather than distress. While I'm sure she found some of the material gross, if not dis-gusting, she wasn't quite sure if it was deviant. The reason for her uncertainty was that, while we may talk to teens about the healthy aspects of sex, we tend not to tell them about ways in which sex can be degrading and abusive. As a result, it's hard for them to know what's healthy and what isn't.

THE NEW STRANGER DANGER

A man approached me during a break in a workshop I was giving on Internet stalking. He explained that he'd come because of a recent tragedy. His good friends' teenage daughter had been forcibly confined and repeatedly raped by a man in his twenties. They had got to know one another on the Internet, and she had agreed to meet him in the relative safety of a crowded public area—a shopping mall. The meeting had been uneventful, although she learned he was somewhat older than he'd claimed to be. She trusted him enough to accept a ride home; this too was uneventful. Days later he knocked on the door after everyone else had left for the day and forced his way in.

Many other examples of Internet luring or "cyberstalking" have appeared in the media. As far as can be determined, while it's common for teens to communicate with strangers on the Internet, only a small number ever meet the person directly. Also, when meetings occur, most don't lead to tragedy. But there are exceptions, and teens need to learn how to protect themselves in cyberspace, just as they have to in the physical world.

Luring can also occur without any direct contact. A 21-year-old student was arrested recently after police received reports he'd abused over 100 girls in North America and Britain. He had contacted the girls through chat rooms, presenting himself as a peer. He persuaded them to use their webcams to send photographs or videos of themselves in sexual poses. Once he had the images in his possession, he threatened to post them on the Internet or send them to family members if the girls didn't engage in cybersex, such as masturbating in front of their webcams.

One consequence of the Internet that receives little attention is the support it gives for deviant behavior, including sexual abuse of minors. Pedophiles have been among society's outcasts. They've been isolated in the past; a pedophile would rarely have contact with anyone who shared his fantasies or preferences. He could hardly publicize his interest in finding like-minded people; such self-disclosure would have been devastating for him socially, as well as alerting the criminal justice system to his presence.

The same freedom of association provided by the Internet that allows people who want to share their love of bottles or Elvis sightings is available to pedophiles. In this way, the Internet ended their isolation and allowed them to form support groups. One such site not only condones pedophilia, it asserts that pedophiles are visionary and want to liberate children from oppression. They call themselves "girllovers," thereby distinguishing themselves from "child molesters." To quote directly from the founder of the Girllovers: "I am not a monster. I am a sensitive and civilized person who has a different sexual orientation than the vast majority of the population. I am interested in beauty and aesthetics, and very deeply want to have the freedom to express my admiration and love for little girls in every way, emotionally, intellectually and sexually."

A frequent question asked at workshops is why we allow such sites to exist. The answer is that, while it's illegal to have sex with a minor, it isn't illegal to have and publicize the opinion that such sex should be permitted, however offensive this may be to the rest of the population.

It would be extremely difficult to determine the extent to which pedophile websites and chat rooms add to the risk of Internet luring, but I'd be surprised if they weren't a factor. They implicitly and explicitly give permission for pedophiles to pursue their interest in having sex with minors. The people who host such sites aren't fools; many are obviously well-educated and they present numerous arguments as to why sex with children is both acceptable and desirable. Such arguments potentially provide pedophiles with material to incorporate in their efforts to gradually and gently persuade a young person that sex with an adult is healthy.

INTERNET BULLYING

I was talking with the vice-principal of an elementary school recently who has become increasingly concerned about bullying on the Internet. This provides another example of an old problem that emerges in a new form. Bullying occurs in many different ways. As discussed in Chapter Eight, boys are more likely to be physically aggressive to one another; girls, on the other hand, are prone to using verbal aggression, as well as social isolation. Given this gender difference, it wasn't surprising to hear that the vice-principal had encountered Internet bullying more frequently among her female students.

Instant messaging allows young people to form social groups, just as they do at school or in their neighborhood. As much as membership can be a source of support and friendship, it can make life miserable. People can turn on one another and establish alliances. If one girl has a grudge, she may be able to recruit supporters, and someone who enjoyed the friendship of the other girls online may suddenly find herself being verbally attacked and eventually isolated in cyberspace. A recent survey found that 14 percent of young people have been threatened while using instant messaging; 16 percent admitted to posting hateful comments themselves.

While the content of Internet bullying isn't new, the potential audience is far greater than could ever have been imagined previously. Launching your own website is no longer a challenging task—at least not for the average cyberkid. A teen can suddenly find himself the subject of a website that can be seen by anyone with Internet access. Just knowing that, in principle, millions of people can read insulting comments about you can be traumatizing. You have no way of knowing who has visited the site, and you may find that students you once thought were friends begin to avoid you at school. If your email address has been posted, you may also start receiving hate mail from complete strangers who believe what has been posted about you and want to join the chorus of bullies.

The anonymity of the Internet can add to the problem. It's bad enough when someone harasses you directly, but at least you know who the person is and have the opportunity to respond in some way. The author of a website, however, is unlikely to reveal his identity. The thought that a nameless and faceless person out there is determined to make your life miserable is unnerving, to say the least.

THE INTERNET PARADOX

The Internet allows contact with countless people, but does it actually promote social growth? This debate follows in the wake of concerns about the impact of being glued to television or mesmerized by video games. The more time is allocated to these leisure pursuits, the less time is available for other things, such as building relationships. It can be argued the Internet is somewhat different if you spend your time meeting people in cyberspace and, in this way, are expanding your social network. The research offers some help in resolving the debate. There are teens who become less involved in direct interaction after their social lives become focused on the Internet. They communicate less with family members in the household, have a diminished social circle, and experience increased feelings of isolation. But this isn't always true. We're finding out that individual differences apply. The more extroverted teen who already has a very active social life can develop an equally active social life on the Internet without any decrease in direct contact with friends. The introverted, shy teen, on the other hand, may instantly feel more comfortable interacting on the Internet, and cyberspace can become his preferred meeting place. Referring to the extroverted teens, one researcher commented, "The rich get richer."

Parents are left with yet a further illustration of the fact that the Internet is neither good nor bad. It's just another tool that can work well for some teens but not so well for others. The time to become concerned and take steps to limit use is when it seems your daughter or son isn't balancing an Internet social life with other relationships. Learning how to feel comfortable and successful in the physical world can sometimes be difficult and stressful, but they can't live in cyberspace forever.

CYBERPROOFING AND CYBERPOLICING

I find it useful to draw a parallel between the physical community and the Internet when talking about ways to protect teens on the Internet. Many of the principles that apply to the physical world can be applied to cyberspace. Parents already have numerous ideas and strategies for protecting their children; all they need do is apply them to the world created by the Internet. Some modification may be necessary, but the principles are much the same.

- **Get yourself up to speed.** Parents are good at teaching their children about the physical community. They accompany them on their excursions from the home, introduce them to the playground, patiently review the etiquette of waiting their turn on the slide, and hold their hand while crossing the road. They teach them how to obtain the information they want at the library and how to behave if a friendly stranger talks to them at the bookshelves. All this, of course, requires communication, and parents who are otherwise confident about their skills have told me they feel at a loss when it comes to talking to their offspring about the Internet.

  The reason is simple. It's exactly the same reason why I can't communicate effectively with my son about the course he's taking in digital logic. I have yet to understand the meaning of the title, let alone engage him in any sensible or meaningful conversation about its contents. Communicating with your daughter or son about the Internet doesn't even get off the ground if you've only recently solved the mystery of how to turn the computer on. But don't despair if you fall into this category. People love to show off what they know; just grab the nearest available child, friend, or neighbor and ask for a 30-minute lesson about the Internet. I personally guarantee the lesson will be more than enough for you to know how to launch a search (this should take less than five minutes) and learn about the different areas and uses of the Internet. Your next step is to find time to sit down in front of the computer and engage in rampant mouse clicking. One final suggestion: one of the best places to learn about the Internet is on the Internet. Just look around your home page (a topic covered in your 30-minute lesson) and you'll find links to all kinds of information about cyberspace, including Internet safety.

- **Think of the Internet as an addition to the list of devices you'll teach your daughter or son to use responsibly and safely.** Other examples are the stove, toaster, scissors, lawn mower, and family car. As is the case for all of these examples, the level of instruction and degree of supervision and monitoring will typically decrease over time. By the time they leave home, however, they should be able to use all these, and many other, tools responsibly. The Internet is no different. Parents begin with careful monitoring. They may post rules by the computer, restrict the number of sites that can be visited, install filters, and check where their children have been on the Internet. As parents become more confident their child can use the Internet safely, parental supervision relaxes.

A common question I receive is whether or not a teenager should have a computer in her bedroom with Internet connection. Quite often the parent has heard this should never be allowed. I jump straight up on the fence, insisting that "maybe" is the only sensible answer—it all depends on her track record. I advocate setting the goal that she'll be able to use the Internet safely by the time she leaves home. If she heads off to college or university, for example, she could easily be one of those students who has to complete parts of her courses online. It's a matter of considering her track record and deciding when the time is right to give her this degree of responsibility.

Another question has been use of webcams, which allow real-time visual communication. They can be part of sexual exploitation. For example, young people have been persuaded to engage in sexual acts such as mutual masturbation in front of webcams. But I see no reason to outlaw this technology. It again illustrates the importance of knowing the dangers and determining when and with what degree of supervision the technology will be used. Going back to an earlier example, a webcam can add to the pleasure of communicating with a distant relative; it can also provide visual information when two students are working together on a school project. Just as you teach your son to be responsible before he uses the stove on his own, you can prepare him to use a webcam so he can enjoy the benefits and avoid the risks.

- **Apply "stranger danger" to the Internet.** Teens need to know the dangers in cyberspace, just as they need to know the dangers in their community. Discussion of topics such as accidental exposure to pornography, the ease with which people can create a false identity, and the reality of Internet luring is in order.

  I recommend highlighting the issue of trust. Most teens are fully aware they shouldn't reveal information such as their address or telephone number to strangers on the Internet. This sounds commendable, but they may nonetheless expose themselves to risk. Teens in one study explained that, after they get to know a person on the Internet, they no longer see him as a "stranger." At this point they can trust him and will divulge more and more personal information. How long does it take for this level of trust to develop? A study conducted by the Media Awareness Network found that it took at most a few weeks, and as little as 15 minutes. As the authors commented, "Not a long time for a skilled predator to wait."

  One reason why teens can be so quick to trust is that most haven't lived in a world that typically threatens or hurts them. We teach them about stranger danger when they're young, but we don't expect them to run and hide whenever they see an unfamiliar face. Another factor is that their image of predators can be faulty. Pedophiles, for example, can present themselves very well in almost all areas of their lives, and they aren't going to advertise their true motive for wanting to form a relationship with a teen. An effective way of emphasizing how hard it is to distinguish predators from other people uses an approach much like the police identification lineups. Students are shown slides of convicted sex offenders mixed in with slides of prominent people they're unlikely to recognize, such as famous authors, company presidents, and foreign heads of state. The success rate of identifying the good guys from the bad is never above chance.

- **Supervise and monitor.** A common recommendation is to ensure that a computer with Internet access is kept in an open area of the home where it's easily monitored by a parent. As I've discussed, I recommend progressively reducing direct supervision as teenagers approach adulthood. For younger children, however, placing the computer in a public area helps ensure the greater level of monitoring required. At the same time, it's important not to be lulled into a false sense of security. Most parents don't have the time to sit with their child continuously. Chances are they'll leave the area periodically to prepare a meal, make a telephone call, put in a load of laundry, or attend to another one of the items on their to-do list. No search for forbidden sites is likely to take more than a few seconds. It will be completed long before the parent has even reached the kitchen.

  One option is to use software that can block sites containing certain key words. A potential problem, however, is that once material is labeled "forbidden fruit" it can become more appealing. This effect was found, for example, in response to warnings about the violent content in television programs. The implication that it might not be a good idea to watch a particular program can increase a young person's motivation to do so. Blocking certain areas of the Internet may have the same effect, and children who are persistent and sophisticated when it comes to surfing may successfully rise to the challenge.

I don't intend to portray children as deviant creatures who are waiting anxiously for a chance to explore the seedy sectors of cyberspace. But they're often curious, and it takes no more than a few seconds to travel to places that are off-limits. An alternative approach is to use discussion and monitoring to encourage teenagers to become their own "censor board," recognizing that they'll soon have full access to almost any type of information they might seek.

Whether or not acquiring material such as pornography will influence young people's behavior is another one of those important questions that's extremely difficult to answer. I suspect I'm in the company of most parents, however, when I express the wish to have some measure of control over the material my children are exposed to. The goal isn't only to shield them but also to retain some influence over their moral reasoning so they can understand how obtaining certain types of information tacitly supports values and practices that offend, denigrate, and hurt others.

Keeping up-to-date with the technology isn't as hard as it may sound. Again, the best place to learn about the current dangers and the most effective safeguards is the Internet itself. Just as there are times when you want to check that your son really did go to a friend's house, there are ways to track the sites he's visited on the Internet. There are also sites where you can be guaranteed the information is of a high quality. For the student who's trying to finish that project on the French Revolution, you can make sure she doesn't end up on my site by directing her to the Internet equivalent of the public library, where material is selected and screened. Some of these "safe sites" include secure places to meet others. While providing chat rooms for teens, they have rules and monitors who enforce them. Inappropriate language or requests for personal identity information can result in the person being blocked from returning.

Let me assure you that becoming comfortable in cyberspace is not that difficult or time-consuming. I'm far from an expert on the

Internet. After typing this sentence, I did a search for "understanding the Internet." One-sixth of a second later I had 105,000 sites to review. I will depart this life never knowing how the system works so quickly. Fortunately, often you don't need a detailed understanding of how something works to use it safely: ignorance of the internal combustion engine isn't an obstacle to safe driving.

The Bibliography has suggestions for gathering more information. Once you get started, you'll find many sources of advice and information geared toward parents who want to teach their children to use the Internet safely. Get clicking!

CHAPTER 12

SINGLE-PARENT AND BLENDED FAMILIES

WHAT IS A FAMILY ANYWAY?

I doubt that I was exactly what my in-laws had in mind for their daughter. I hasten to add that I've never resented this; after all, name one parent you know who has said, "When you grow up, try to marry a divorced man with children so you can become a stepmother on your wedding day." So when Kathy told her parents she was dating a single father, I can appreciate why signs of apprehension, shock, and dismay were obvious, while indications of acceptance and enthusiasm weren't. Her parents always placed great value on education and the fact that I had a PhD helped, but they'd have gladly settled for a BA and no kids.

Most of us have grown up with the idea that a normal family consists of a mother and father, plus one or more offspring. The question "what is a family?" wouldn't have been asked a generation ago. Death, and sometimes divorce, led to single-parent homes and stepfamilies, but these situations were very much exceptions; the two-parent, biological family ruled supreme as the model of family life. When we were young and fantasized about our futures, most of us saw ourselves continuing to live in a nuclear family, only as the parents rather than the children.

Then the divorce rate skyrocketed. Estimates vary, but anywhere from one-third to almost one-half of marriages can be expected to fail. Another way of describing the changes that have occurred is by referring to the statistics directly concerning children. For example, almost half of the children born in the eighties will spend at least part of their childhood in a single-parent family. As for blended families, the projection is that approximately one-third of children can expect to be part of such homes by the turn of the century. Whatever statistic is used, the conclusion has to be that the nuclear family no longer has such an exclusive, dominant role in society.

EXPECTATIONS AND THE SECOND-RATE MYTH

Before discussing specific issues relating to day-to-day parenting of teens in single-parent and blended families I'd like to address the severe attitude problem that tends to be prevalent among their members. This is based on certain misguided expectations. One particularly powerful type of expectation is the self-fulfilling prophecy. This refers to the idea that if we expect to find a task too difficult, this increases the likelihood we'll fail; conversely, anticipating that we'll do well increases the likelihood of success. Much of the early interest in self-fulfilling prophecies related to education. For example, there are studies suggesting that one reason some students may not achieve academically is simply that less is expected of them. There are, of course, limits to the power of self-fulfilling prophecies; ability is a factor as well. Part of my midlife crisis was to rekindle my fantasy of being a saxophone player in a blues band. I analyzed the situation and determined there were only two obstacles: no saxophone and no talent. While I was able to overcome the first, my music teacher and I quickly decided the second would almost certainly be a lifelong condition.

Parents in blended and single-parent families are often victims of a negative self-fulfilling prophesy; this is based on the belief they're inferior to the more traditional nuclear family. They come by this attitude problem honestly, as society seems intent on viewing their version of family life as second-rate; while there may be an increasing acceptance of different types of families, this doesn't necessarily mean they're held in particularly high regard. For example, it wasn't that long ago that a well-known dictionary defined a stepchild as "one who fails to receive proper care or attention." That's pretty insulting and unforgivably presumptuous, but it reflects the common myth that being in a stepfamily is, of necessity, second-rate. Single-parent families haven't fared any better. As summarized in an article by Bonnie Barber at Pennsylvania State University and her colleague, Jacquelynne Eccles, such families are considered "incomplete and are frequently seen as primary contributors to delinquency, poor academic performance, dropping out of school, negative relationships with parents, decreased self-esteem, sexual promiscuity, and welfare dependence." That's quite a list and hardly gives single parents any hope for their children's future.

Fortunately, the belief that there's something intrinsic to blended and single-parent families that makes them less effective proves to be another example of the dangers of making assumptions. This is where the research is helpful, although it's also complex. First of all, the results vary according to the particular area of development or adjustment being studied. Second, as so often happens in the social sciences, not everyone gets the same results even when they ask much the same question. An example is provided by the studies of self-concept. This is an important area as most parents obviously attach a great deal of importance to their children's ability to see themselves as worthwhile and likable people who enjoy the self-confidence that such a perception permits.

Numerous studies have been conducted in which the self-concepts of children in nuclear and blended and single-parent families have been compared. No consistent differences have emerged. One researcher may find that children from nuclear families score higher on measures of self-esteem; another may fail to find such a difference. Similarly, there's a lack of consistency in the research concerning academic achievement and general measures of personal adjustment. Other research has examined the impact of economic factors. For example, most single parents are women and are likely to be in relatively low-paying jobs. Those single-parent families that are more financially secure, however, tend to encounter fewer difficulties. This finding has led researchers to conclude that lack of financial resources, rather than the structure of the family itself, is a major reason why some children are more vulnerable.

Some studies have even indicated blended or single-parent families can confer certain advantages. For example, stepchildren may be at an advantage with respect to social skills, perhaps because they need to learn how to develop new and more complex relationships than typically exist in other families. And studies have reported that teenagers from single-parent families can be more independent and responsible than their peers in nuclear families, possibly because they may be expected, if not required, to take on more family responsibilities since most single parents work outside the home. Finally, studies specifically examining the impact of employment on single-parent families have found that it can enhance the children's self-esteem and lead to their being less restricted by gender stereotypes in their vocational aspirations. Such findings fly in the face of the notion that single, employed parents couldn't possibly be taking adequate care of their children.

It's also important to keep in mind that when studies have found a higher incidence of problems among children from blended or single-parent families, the magnitude of the differences is typically small. For example, Doctors Zimiles and Lee from Michigan studied over 13,000 students and found lower achievement scores and higher dropout rates among students from stepfamilies. The way I've chosen to describe their findings is accurate, but it could leave you with the feeling that being in a stepfamily condemns you to a life of ignorance and underachievement. Yet, the same findings could be described in a far more positive and optimistic way. As the researchers pointed out in their article, the achievement scores for students from nuclear families were higher by a "comparatively small margin." It was also true that while students from stepfamilies were more likely to drop out, a substantial majority didn't.

There's no doubt that most blended and single-parent families have to deal with significant challenges. The research tells us, however, that membership in such a family isn't the same as being sentenced to life with no chance of parole. The myth of being second-rate results in people feeling stuck and inadequate; the more realistic view creates the expectation that their children will grow up to be well-adjusted adults, even though achieving this goal may be harder and more stressful at times.

JUST FOR BLENDED FAMILIES

WRITING YOUR OWN SCRIPT

A young couple will have preconceived notions about courtship, engagement, and marriage, as will their families and friends and society at large. This script doesn't have to be adhered to rigidly; there's plenty of room for improvisation, but the couple is likely to retain a general understanding of how their life together will unfold. Members of stepfamilies don't have the benefit of such guidelines. What is a stepfamily *supposed* to look like, and how is it *supposed* to function? Stepfamilies vary so much in their structure and histories that it would never be possible to write a single script for them to follow. This is particularly true if the stepfamily is formed when the children are older. Close relationships *may* develop, but it isn't uncommon for stepparents and their adolescent stepchildren to remain at the level of "sociable, polite strangers." Similarly, while some stepparents eventually become authority figures without this causing unnecessary conflict in the family, others find it better to remain in the back seat.

While there are no acceptable guidelines for stepfamilies, just a smattering of rationalization allows me to argue that this affords them a great deal of power and flexibility. Not having a ready-made script means that parents and children can assume the responsibility for determining which guidelines best suit their family given their particular wishes and circumstances.

YOU CAN'T TELL ME WHAT TO DO

Sooner or later most stepparents will be reminded they aren't a "real" parent. Not that stepparents are unaware of the lack of biological connection; it's just that stepchildren like to keep this piece of information as a trump card to be played at opportune moments. The standard form is, "You're not my mother; you can't tell me what to do." Rarely do you hear, "You're not my mother; you can't drive me to the mall," or "I don't have to eat these home-baked chocolate chip cookies; you're not my father."

A question that becomes particularly important to resolve for the family with teenagers is the extent to which a stepparent should become involved in discipline. In reaching this decision, it can be helpful to think about how the two primary roles of parents evolve; these roles are nurturing and guidance. An essential part of the latter role is exercising discipline. In nuclear families parents readily combine the two roles. The parent who hugs her daughter when she returns from school may scold her on discovering that yet another glove has been donated to the lost and found box. A teenager may look for reassurance from a parent about how he looks before going out to a dance, only to be grounded the same evening for ignoring his curfew.

Because biological parents typically have the responsibility for both nurturing and discipline, stepparents can often feel they're supposed to follow suit. In some stepfamilies, this can become a guaranteed way of creating conflict, particularly if the stepparent arrives when the children are adolescents. Historically, however, parents in nuclear families don't immediately assume both roles for the simple reason that there's almost no need to discipline infants. With very few exceptions, a baby's behavior is accepted for what it is. The mother obviously doesn't establish limits regarding how many diaper changes are permissible or impose consequences for crying or waking up in the night. The baby's extreme dependency and helplessness permit the parent to have a great deal of control. It's only when the infant gets older and begins to have choices regarding what she'll do that the question of who will be in charge is opened up for debate. So the first year or so can be almost exclusively a period of nurturing. It's a time when the infant is fed, cuddled, rocked, bathed, and sung to, as well as all those other wonderful things that help the emotional bond become strong and secure.

The child's acceptance of the parent's right to guide and discipline follows this period of attachment. In many instances, however, the stepparent hasn't had the opportunity to form this type of attachment. The question to be decided, therefore, is how much involvement there should be in matters of discipline.

A starting point is to consider the merits of the stepparent having as little direct responsibility for discipline as possible. The Fosters were a stepfamily I became quite attached to, but preferred to see fairly late in the evening to avoid disturbing other people in the building. Abby was one of those girls I'd love to have as a grandchild; her energy, humor, warmth, and self-confidence would endear her to me between two and five on a Sunday afternoon, but her belief that the age of majority should be lowered to 12 would make her a challenge to parent. The concerns expressed in the family were mainly behavioral; it wasn't that Abby was seen as a bad child, she was just very difficult and argumentative. Her mother would give an example of a conflict; almost immediately Abby would provide a loud and contradictory version of what had happened. As the stepfather moved in to support his wife, however, the topic would be changed rapidly to that of whether or not he was entitled to have any say in what she did. Abby had a seemingly endless number of variations of the "you're not my father" line, and each one prompted a renewed but ineffective attempt on the stepfather's part to assert his authority. As daughter and stepfather locked horns yet again, the rest of the family and I became the audience.

We scheduled a cabinet meeting—just the parents, Jim and Debbie, and myself. I'm particular about how these are orchestrated. The whole family was invited, but I asked the parents to instruct Abby and her younger brother to stay in the waiting room while we had a meeting. Some family therapists call this "boundary making"; it's a way of reinforcing the idea that sometimes parents have to make decisions that are passed down to the children. I like it because it drives the kids crazy not knowing what we're up to; a well-placed measure of anxiety can be a great therapeutic tool. Behind closed doors we talked about possible ways of changing the organization in the family. Debbie and Jim brought up the issue of the right to discipline. I have no argument with the position that, as an adult in the family, a stepparent has the right to more power and influence than the children. But while Jim had the right to assume a disciplinary role, he also had the right to a long life and happiness. The former was in jeopardy and the latter was clearly being violated. He couldn't give any other example of a job he'd accepted that offered no pleasure, no pay, and no hope of advancement. While I felt it premature to ask him to resign, I suggested he and Debbie think about a temporary leave of absence.

The recommendation to parents that they do less or nothing is always the hardest to make. When families are struggling with a problem, they want to actively work toward a solution. What helped Jim and Debbie decide to accept the recommendation, however, was their awareness that the battles over who had the right to discipline were getting them nowhere, as well as making it almost impossible for Jim to enjoy the time he spent with Abby. The conflicts also obscured issues that needed to be dealt with in the family. Instead of the much-needed negotiation regarding what rules, incentives, and consequences should be in place, they were stuck on the question of who should be at the bargaining table.

A new position for Jim was established. He was hired primarily as Debbie's consultant. She'd have the final say but would ask his opinion at times, just as he'd offer his whenever he felt so inclined. It was Debbie, however, who'd deal directly with Abby on all matters concerning discipline whenever possible. If problems arose when Debbie wasn't present, Jim would remind Abby of what her mother would expect her to do. If necessary, he'd tell her that he'd let her mother know if she decided to ignore the rules. He'd only move in to take over control in dire emergencies; otherwise, Abby was answerable to her mother.

The understanding that, although Debbie was responsible for discipline, Jim would voice his opinions at times allowed him a measure of indirect power. The expectation that a stepparent will speak only when spoken to can create its own set of problems; it can be very stressful to live with children who have habits and behaviors you feel should be added to the Criminal Code. It would be most unusual for a parent and stepparent to start with the same standards for children's behavior, and regular cabinet meetings may be necessary to effect a compromise between the existing regime and the stepparent's views and wishes. Ideally, however, any changes that are decided upon will be implemented gradually; resentment is likely to be fostered if the stepparent is seen as the one who makes the rules, even though he may not be the enforcer.

Back to Abby, who was ushered into the cabinet room, obviously wanting to know what we'd been plotting but doing her best to feign complete indifference. We went through formal introductions, whereby each member of the family was given a job description. Her mother explained her position, including her role as the authority figure; Jim explained his. I added that Abby's task was to find another technique for diverting attention away from her behavior. Without any opposition to the "you're not my father" statement, she was defenseless. I'm sure she worked hard to find one, but once diversionary tactics have been labeled as such in a family, they tend to lose their effectiveness.

Sometimes family therapy can seem manipulative. The intention, however, is to enact what needs to happen in the family. Excluding children from discussions often has the goal of helping them become closer to parents. Over time, Abby began to change her view of her stepfather as a sparring partner. This allowed her to develop healthier ways of relating to him, and it was obviously a source of much pleasure for them both to find they could actually enjoy one another's company on occasion.

When comparisons have been made of stepfamilies who feel they've been successful and those who don't, significant differences have been found in the extent of the stepparent's involvement in discipline and other aspects of decision-making that relate to the stepchildren. By and large, success is associated with either minimal involvement or a very gradual increase in assuming these types of responsibilities. If a stepparent isn't bringing children into the home, this lack of involvement can seem unfair. After all, marriage is supposed to involve sharing, and if your spouse has single-handedly coped with the daily demands and stresses of child-rearing, shouldn't you be willing to help out? While this logic can't be faulted, the advantages of sharing a task can quickly vanish if the result is a level of tension and conflict in the home that's taking the joy out of family life.

Another concern can be that lack of involvement in discipline will maintain the stepparent's peripheral role and make it harder for her to become a full member of the family. The opposite is probably true in most situations. Acceptance and attachment are more likely to develop when emphasis is placed on allowing the stepparent and children to gradually get to know one another. Just as instant love is an unrealistic expectation, so is instant respect as an authority figure. Assuming this role too quickly can create a level of conflict and resentment that impedes rather than fosters the relationship between the stepparent and stepchild.

I have to return to the principle that no one script applies to all stepfamilies. Situations will exist in which it's very difficult for the stepparent to avoid taking an active role in discipline. The biological parent may be absent from the home because of shift work or the need to travel on business, and the stepparent will be left to manage the household on a regular basis. It's nonetheless possible for the biological parent to retain much of the responsibility for establishing the rules. The family can sit down together to discuss matters relating to discipline, and children can be made aware that although the stepparent has an influence on the decisions that are made, they are, above all, accountable to their biological parent. A parallel in the work force is the expectation that when the boss is absent, she'll delegate someone to be in charge. This person may need to interpret the policies and procedures but won't change them or establish new ones.

Issues concerning discipline can become more complicated when both parents bring children into the stepfamily. I'd still advocate the same starting point: one parent disciplines his children; the other disciplines hers. In this situation, however, changes may need to occur more rapidly than in a stepfamily in which only one parent has children. It would be unusual to find two parents who have exactly the same attitudes toward child-rearing. Although the research has yet to be conducted, I'm confident that if you asked two single parents why they'd fallen madly in love, sharing the same ideas regarding how children should behave at the meal table or how much allowance they should receive wouldn't be high on the list of reasons. If the parenting styles and expectations are close, family life can proceed with the children being answerable primarily to their respective biological parents. Tension and dissatisfaction can arise, however, if the differences between the parenting styles are pronounced. A 14-year-old boy may have had no difficulty accepting a 10 o'clock bedtime but will be incited to mutiny on learning that his 13-year-old stepsister can decide when to go to bed. Similarly, having the task of doing the dishes regularly will no longer be seen as fair if it seems your stepbrother's only job is to dirty them.

The more the two parents differ in their approaches and expectations, the more likely it is that one will be seen as unjust and too strict. This can create a great deal of conflict, and the decision may be made to move toward a middle ground so there can be more consistency with respect to discipline. This requires embarking on a process of negotiation and compromise in which both parents should have equal power and in which neither approach is assumed to be superior to the other. If one parent is perceived as the victor because of successfully asserting his practices and beliefs, he can become a ready target for his stepchildren's resentment. Open discussion in which the children participate and hear the parents express mutual respect and reach joint decisions can make it far easier for all members of the family to accept changes in how the home is to be structured and managed. The principle that each child is answerable to her biological parent can remain. As in any stepfamily, this may change over time, but it may not. A stepparent's gradual assumption of equal responsibility for discipline is best seen as a possibility, not a requirement.

DO I HAVE TO LIKE YOU?

The unwritten rulebook for parents states they should love their children. I wouldn't question the validity of this expectation for nuclear families; it would also apply to single parents. Too often, however, parents and stepfamilies try to use it as well. For very understandable reasons they want a close home life but find out all too soon that you can't just add a new parent, mix well, and have an instant loving family. No more than a moment's reflection should be sufficient to dismiss this instant love myth. How often do any of us experience such an automatic and strong bonding? Each time I tell the story of how I met Kathy on a camping trip I change and embellish many of the details, but I always include the part where she first spied me, an Adonis-like figure silhouetted against the setting sun, and fell hopelessly and instantly in love. (Kathy also applies the word "hopeless" in her account of the meeting, though in a very different context.)

When I leave the realm of personal fantasy I'm left with only the experience of childbirth as a credible example of instant love. Something unique and very special can happen when a parent first holds and cradles a child after birth, and in nuclear families the relationships with the children have the advantage of this strong bonding. Compare the experience of holding a newborn to that of picking your boyfriend up from his house and meeting his teenage daughter for the first time. Her greeting, "Hi! Nice to meet you," may sound reassuring, but her tone and manner may be telling you, "Mess with my dad, lady, and I'll break your face." Both of you are probably experiencing strong and instant emotions, but love is unlikely to be one of them.

One of the biggest unknowns for stepfamilies is the extent to which emotional attachments will form. I could predict that a child in a nuclear family would have a strong bond with her biological parents, but I somehow doubt you'd be impressed by my insight and powers of prophecy. I'd be far less willing to offer an opinion as to whether or not a child is likely to become emotionally attached to a stepparent. My best answer—"maybe"— would also fail to enhance my reputation as a soothsayer.

I like to suggest that parents take the time to discuss what kind of relationships they hope will develop and compare this to the type of relationship they feel will be realistic. Often these aren't the same when the relationship didn't begin when the stepchild was very young. A boy entering his adolescence and at the same time joining a stepfamily can be faced with two opposing forces. An essential part of adolescence is preparing to move away from the family; this maturational process provides young people with the drive to become independent and their parents with the hope of peace in their old age. But if the stepson is expected to develop an increasingly close relationship with the stepfather, he's confronted with the task of moving closer and moving away at the same time. The conflict that's created can be intense and hard to resolve. Establishing a more realistic goal for the relationship that doesn't require this level of closeness can ease the conflict considerably.

I suggest that stepfamilies create the expectation that the relationship between stepparents and older stepchildren will be allowed to develop slowly. Put another way, you can try to speed things up, but you can't escape the fact that when people in a relationship want to move at different speeds, it's the slower one who sets the pace. Recognizing this leads many stepparents to adopt the view that they should allow their stepchildren to come to them. It can be very difficult to know when a stepchild is ready to move closer to you emotionally, but the likelihood this will occur is increased when he knows that such movement would be welcomed but isn't demanded or necessarily anticipated.

It can be helpful to think in terms of years rather than months. Even for young children, one study found that it took up to two years before several stepfathers felt they had a comfortable relationship with their stepchildren. When the stepchildren are older, it may well take much longer; estimates of five years aren't unusual when people write about the process of establishing a solid relationship with adolescent stepchildren.

Provided the stepparent has some input into discipline, the early phase of the relationship can be viewed as similar to the beginning of a friendship. An obvious part of friendship is being willing to do things for the other person. In any family there's no shortage of tasks to be taken on, ranging from cooking meals and helping with school projects to providing taxi services and repairing toys. Another part of friendship is enjoying time together. This may be more challenging; it can be much easier to find something to do *for* an adolescent stepchild than something to do *with* them. Remembering that there are many degrees of togetherness can be helpful. Watching a stepson's basketball game may not exactly be intimate, but at least the two of you are in the same place and sharing the experience. At some point you may enjoy sitting together to watch a game on television and move on to taking practice shots against each other in the driveway, but all in good time.

Stepparents can become frustrated when the relationship seems to be moving at a slow pace, or perhaps not moving at all. At such times there can be some comfort to be had from the research. Stepfamilies that pass tests of adjustment and global satisfaction with flying colors tend to report two things. The first is that emotional attachments have developed slowly; presumably they allowed the pace to be leisurely so the stepchildren were less likely to get anxious or threatened from feeling the stepparent was trying to move into their lives too quickly. The second is that success wasn't necessarily associated with having close relationships; it seems a number of stepfamilies reach the stage when they see themselves as secure and well-adjusted even though stepparents and stepchildren are more than content to view themselves as acquaintances or casual friends.

A relationship that feels stuck may denote a problem, but it can also be the case that the relationship has reached the level of its potential, at least for the time being. Enjoying it for what it is will be far more profitable than lamenting what it hasn't—and perhaps can never—become.

Parallels between a friendship and stepparenting exist, but there are also noticeable differences. Friendships are usually reciprocal; we expect our interest in the other person will be met with similar enthusiasm. If I find I'm the only one who calls the other person or suggests we get together, I'll eventually come to the realization that he finds my company less than stimulating. I can then look elsewhere to try to cultivate friendships. Stepparents aren't in this position. They can't trade in their stepchildren if their overtures of interest, affection, and friendship are met with yawns, derisive laughter, or a turned back.

Sam and Regina Vuchinich at Oregon State University and their colleagues observed videotapes of 26 stepfamilies in which there were early adolescent children. Each family was taped while they were eating supper. Two years later they returned to have another look. Their interest was in evaluating how members of stepfamilies interact—particularly stepfathers and their stepchildren.

It could be argued that having a video camera pointed at the table wouldn't only stop people from eating their chicken with their fingers but would also ensure that a facade of politeness is maintained, even when a food fight was the norm. This rarely seems to happen, however; inhibitions are usually temporary and chances are good that the behavior observed will be representative of family life.

The researchers rated the videotapes in several ways. For example, they noted prosocial behavior such as compliments; oppositional behavior such as disagreements and insults; and commands, questions, and answers. Interactions could then be coded. A stepfather's question, "How do you like my casserole?" followed by his stepdaughter's answer, "I hope they bury the recipe with you— tomorrow," would be coded question-answer/opposition.

I want to mention just a few of the results. They noted that stepfathers seemed to be making a "sustained effort to develop better relationships with their stepchildren" over the two-year period.

Their adolescent children, on the other hand, seemed to be making a sustained effort to ignore these overtures. This was especially true for the girls. It wasn't that the stepchildren were typically out-and-out obnoxious; they just tended to ignore their stepfathers or responded to them with barely a flicker of life.

What amazed me was that the stepfathers were still plugging away with questions like "did you have a good day at school?" and "how's your dinner?" Presumably they'd adopted a view that a grunt in return would be a major breakthrough. I should add that biological parents may be no strangers to this type of one-way street with their adolescents; it seems, however, that stepparents are more likely to find themselves in this position.

I offer no ready solution. In general, part of being a stepparent is often to invest a lot more than you feel is ever returned. To some extent, stepparents have to live with this inequity and imbalance, and many find they need particularly thick skins if they're to survive without reacting too personally to their daily ration of rejection. On a more optimistic note, they may eventually see more of a return than anticipated. The extent of the child's appreciation for the stepparent may not emerge until later—possibly not until adulthood. While still growing up, there may be too much in the way—for example, confusion regarding allegiances to the step- and biological parents; reluctance to move too close to the stepparent because of fears he, too, may leave; or concentrating on belonging to a peer group rather than forming new family ties. Avoiding chronic frustration requires a willingness to adjust the goals for the relationship so expectations aren't too different from those of the stepchild. As well as accepting that progress will be slow, stepparents should set modest goals and understand that the investment is long-term.

JUST FOR SINGLE-PARENT FAMILIES

IT'S LONELY AT THE TOP

It's no more possible to generalize about single-parent families than it is stepfamilies. Some parents have always been single, and their children have never experienced living in a two-parent family.

Other single-parent families follow the death of a parent. More commonly, however, loss of a parent is the result of divorce. When this is the case, the other parent may remain actively involved; a significant number, however, will progressively become less involved in their children's lives.

Whatever the history of the family, all single parents have to take on the major or exclusive responsibility for raising their children. This can become particularly challenging during the teenage years.

The period following a separation can be especially difficult. Single parents aren't dealing only with the emotional impact of separation themselves but also have the responsibility of helping their children deal with the dramatic changes in family life. The fact that most single parents are women adds to the potential stress, as they tend to have lower-paying employment than their ex spouses.

Martha Hetherington at the University of Virginia has contributed a great deal to our understanding of the impact of separation and divorce on children and parents. She talks about the likelihood that the single parent will go through a period in which she struggles to deal with the impact of marital breakdown and will be less available to her children emotionally and more inclined to be lax with respect to discipline and supervision. The children are also facing a very difficult period in their lives and are prone to being noncompliant, demanding, and dependent. As Dr. Hetherington succinctly comments, this is "not a very winning combination."

Before the picture becomes too gloomy, let me emphasize that the situation tends to improve; as is often the case, the impact of traumatic and stressful events usually dissipates over time. Recognizing how the changes in parenting may be having a negative effect on the family, however, provides a guideline for taking steps to hasten the positive trend. The more quickly single parents can take charge and establish themselves as the head of the family, the sooner any problems with their children are likely to subside. It's useful to evoke the principles of democracy once again.

n of prime minister or president in a nuclear family is
shared; in a single-parent family, however, the position
ly resembles the political world: the ultimate power is
one person.

f my tasks when I'm working with single parents is to
them to ignore me. It isn't just that I like to be reminded
of home; it's because I want to discourage their wish to have my
approval when they make decisions. Although there are times when
my opinion will be asked for directly, the request for my support is
often more subtle. Andrew's mother, Anne, was an articulate person who had no difficulty expressing her disapproval of her teenage
son's antagonistic and defiant behavior toward her. She also made it
clear that she didn't appreciate the way in which he and his younger
sister, Katie, joined forces to challenge her authority. But Anne's
willingness to voice her concerns was accompanied by a lack of confidence that was evident from her habit of frequently looking in my
direction as if to ask me to support what she'd said. At other times
she'd also look to her children for this approval, almost desperately
wanting them to let her know they agreed with her opinions and
decisions. I had no idea if Katie or Andrew recognized the need for
their mother to become more of an authority figure in the family,
but I was confident that neither would admit it if they did.

Anne's difficulty asserting herself was partly the result of that
perennial obstacle to effective parenting—guilt. She knew there
were times when she was preoccupied with her own feelings of
loss; she was also very sensitive to the impact of the loss on her
children. "Getting tough" was, therefore, so easily seen by her as
being mean and insensitive, and her ambivalence about asserting
her authority had led to a failure to establish and adhere to clear
expectations and consequences.

One of our sessions became like a seminar in graduate school.
I believe Anne found some comfort from our discussion of studies indicating that her difficulties asserting herself were common
among single parents in similar situations. The finding that single mothers are particularly likely to have discipline problems

with their sons also rang true for her. As the seminar progressed, Andrew and Katie were, of course, propelled to new heights of boredom, although I'm sure they suspected that trouble was on its way. I believe I was successful in convincing Anne that the research indicated she'd only earn the right to heap more guilt upon herself if she continued to let her kindness and sympathy prevent her from being the authority figure her children required. Having a parent who can take charge as needed is known to help adolescents' adjustment. It also matters little if decisions need to be revised. Anne didn't have the advantage of another parent with whom executive decisions could be reached. She would, therefore, need to get used to making mistakes on her own. Her counterparts in the political sphere have established the precedent that getting it right the first time isn't a requirement of the job, so why should she be different?

CUTTING CORNERS

One of the reasons why single parents can find themselves overwhelmed by the demands of raising their teenagers is no more complex than the fact they're overworked. Traditional models of family life were based on the assumption there would be two parents, one of whom stayed at home. The relevance of such models for modern family life is questionable even when there are two parents; when the parent is single and also employed outside the home, such models become almost irrelevant. Too often, however, single parents seem determined to demonstrate they can be super-parents and do it all. Some may accomplish this goal, but I suspect most find themselves exhausted, frustrated, and feeling as if they've failed.

When I give workshops for single parents I endeavor to persuade them that while they have the right to remain on a path that promises nothing but premature aging and burnout, they might want to consider an alternative direction. I ask them to go through their weekly routines and write a list of activities that are *essential* for the family—for example, going to work, making sure schoolwork is completed, and having time with their children. Never once do I recall seeing vacuuming on the list. This observation led to my founding SAVED (the Society for the Abolition of Vacuuming Every Day). In my efforts to solicit membership dues, I reassure parents that my search of the clinical literature has failed to locate a single study that establishes a link between how often a house is vacuumed and the long-term adjustment of children. Membership is growing.

We go on to talk about other ways of reducing their workload. Not only can some tasks be eliminated or reduced, others can be shared. Teenagers can learn to cook. In fact, there's no household task that's beyond the capabilities of the average adolescent. If they can single-handedly learn the complexities of surfing the Internet or programming the VCR, surely they can master the complexities of a washer and dryer or microwave oven.

Sometimes parents worry they'd be placing an unfair burden on their teenagers by recruiting them into the family work force and will thus rob them of what little is left of their childhood. Family therapists will talk about the dangers of creating a "parental child"— one who has taken on too much of the role that would otherwise be assumed by a spouse. The increased responsibilities for contributing to the day-to-day workings of the home are accompanied by the expectation that the child become the parent's confidant and main source of emotional support. Resentment results from the fact that they have far more information about the parent's personal life than they either want or can deal with adequately; it can also stem from the likelihood that the parent is preoccupied with her own needs to the point where she isn't paying sufficient attention to those of her children. Provided the single parent is careful to ensure this process isn't happening, however, there's a lot to be gained from involving older children more in the running of the home. When I read about the higher levels of maturity, independence, and responsibility that have been found among adolescents in single-parent families, I'm left wondering if those in two-parent households are pampered.

One of the articles I read during my family therapy training discussed the value of involving teenagers in the running of a single-parent home when there were younger siblings. The author pointed out that, back in the days when it wouldn't be unusual for parents to have six or more children, it was considered normal for the older siblings to share responsibility for the care of the younger family members. She also used the analogy of a political democracy, referring to the establishment of a cabinet in which the single parent was the prime minister while the older children were junior ministers. She wasn't naive in suggesting this title; no teenager is going to beam with pleasure at the prospect of ministerial status when all this entails is the right to do the laundry and wash the kitchen floor. Being in the cabinet also meant having a junior role in decision-making—perhaps being consulted about matters concerning the day-to-day running of the house and being asked for an opinion when deciding how to spend money that had been saved to replace old furniture and decorations. She used the term "junior ministers" to highlight the importance of guidance and supervision—to remind the parent that in spite of the benefits of becoming more independent, teenagers still need to feel they can depend on her for support, understanding, and direction. With this in mind, the cabinet meetings wouldn't just be for the purpose of assigning duties or reaching decisions, they'd also create an opportunity for the parent to focus on the needs of her ministers.

TAKING CARE OF YOURSELF

Too often single parents don't see the connection between taking care of themselves and taking care of their children. Single mothers, in particular, risk feeling increasingly lonely, isolated, and trapped. Furthermore, their emotional well-being can have a profound impact on the family as a whole. The decrease in the consistency and effectiveness of discipline that can arise after separation, for example, appears to be at least partly the result of the depression parents can experience during this difficult time. I hasten to add that I'm not trying to suggest single parents who are going through a stressful period of readjustment should "get over it" so they can focus on their children. If it were that simple, they'd have done so without any advice from me.

My objective is to encourage single parents to recognize that taking whatever steps are possible to care for themselves offers the bonus of helping their children. Something as simple as maintaining or reestablishing ties with the extended family, for example, can ease the parent's feelings of depression and loneliness. This, in turn, can increase the effectiveness of parenting. Ronald Taylor and his fellow researchers at Temple University reported that "kinship support" helped single parents to maintain more authoritative styles of parenting, which had predictably positive effects on the adjustment of their adolescent children. There may also be more direct benefits for teenage girls; given the opportunity, they're more likely than boys to view extended family members, such as cousins, grandparents, aunts and uncles, as providing support and warmth. For those parents who don't have a supportive extended family, connecting with community groups can be a means of combating their feelings of isolation.

The parent who decides she wants to further her education and embark on a career isn't neglecting her children; there are ample studies to support the view that such a step can have a positive effect on the quality of life in the family. As always, there's no simple way to sum up the research. Many factors must be considered when evaluating the impact of maternal employment on single-parent families. For instance, parents' satisfaction with their work is relevant to the overall health of the family; it has an obvious effect on their feelings of satisfaction and well-being, which in turn influences the quality of their parenting. Income level is also a major factor; the association between lack of money and poor adjustment among members of single-parent families has been a consistent finding over the years. The trends in education and employment may, therefore, reduce the impact of the financial disadvantages faced by many single parents.

A number of the studies often cited in the field date back several years; moreover, the data analyzed would typically be obtained two to three years before publication of the article. In contrast to the eighties or nineties, women are now more likely to be high school, college, or university graduates. Women in their twenties have no difficulty competing against their male peers with respect to their qualifications, and while gender discrimination in the work force remains, the higher levels of skilled employment aren't as dominated by men as has been the case. Obstacles remain. Women are still more likely than men to have put their education or careers on hold to raise children, and returning to school or employment while simultaneously caring for children is no easy task. But the trend toward higher achievement among women can only help the children in single-parent families enjoy the benefits associated with being raised by someone who has the satisfaction and financial status that comes from meaningful employment.

CHAPTER 13

PUSH COMES TO SHOVE

THE NEED TO BREAK AWAY

Children get very little privacy. If a five-year-old is alone somewhere in the house—and particularly if she's quiet—we tend to suspect something is going on and will launch an investigation. If a two-and-a-half-year-old is alone and quiet we *know* there's something going on and use the "whatever you're doing—don't!" approach, even though the assumption of guilt may seem like trampling on her civil rights.

We don't allow young people very many opportunities to be away from us. During their early years they remain extremely dependent on the family. For the 18-month-old, the home can be a dangerous environment. He can fall down stairs, tumble off furniture, pull pots off the stove, choke on small objects, and slip in the bathtub. We childproof our homes as best we can, but keep our toddlers close to us most of the time.

As they grow up we probably provide fewer opportunities for them to be away from adult supervision than has been the case in previous generations. Ensuring that children are rarely far away from adults is, of course, motivated not only by the wish to protect them. There are also many things they can't do for themselves. Consider the 18-month-old again: he needs someone to change, wash, dress, and feed him. Doors need to be opened, toys have to be lifted down from shelves, and books have to be read. And while we encourage children to become more independent, the idea that they require our help rightly persists. Showing them how to use a spoon is replaced by trying to teach them what to eat in order to be healthy. Instruction regarding dress progresses from doing up your own buttons to how to dress for school and not invite ridicule.

Eventually we need to become far less involved in teaching and directing our offspring. By the time they leave school we want them to have reached the point where they're ready to live independently. This requires a process of separating in which adolescents, in some respects, push away to decrease dependency on parents. As reliance on the family decreases, teenagers become more involved in the community in which they'll be expected to function independently in a few years.

Separating involves establishing an identity. Being a distinct and unique person becomes very important, as does belonging to other groups apart from the family. Without these bridges, leaving home can be a frightening and lonely prospect.

The task of separating is also quite complex: it requires achieving independence and developing strong ties to the community on the one hand while maintaining some connection to the family on the other. Research tells us this balance has an impact on emotional and behavioral adjustment. The message to parents is that they don't become redundant when their sons and daughters begin to establish support systems with their peers. In fact, teens who rely on their friends but don't see their parents as a continuing part of their support system are more likely to experience adjustment difficulties.

CLIQUES, CROWDS, AND FRIENDSHIPS

To learn more about the way teenagers group themselves, field researchers have gatecrashed parties, attended rock concerts, and eaten countless burgers in fast-food restaurants. I make no attempt to mask my envy and admiration of social scientists who have managed to get agencies to fund them to relive their adolescence; as a result of their dedication we know more about the way teenagers group themselves and how these groupings tend to change over the course of adolescence.

One distinction made is between cliques and crowds. Cliques are tight social groups that have relatively few members. The emphasis is on intimacy; a forum is established for sharing opinions, exploring feelings, and providing mutual support. Developing close relationships outside the family can, however, seem very threatening. You need to know that you'll be safe if you let down your guard and begin allowing others to see your doubts and insecurities. So membership in cliques is regulated pretty carefully. This is fine once you're in, but obtaining membership can be difficult. First of all, cohesiveness gets harder to maintain if the clique is too big, so you may have to wait for a vacancy. Second, any would-be members have to be screened meticulously to ensure they have similar interests, values, and social standing. We use the term "cliquish" to refer to the more negative aspects of this type of grouping—in particular, the cold and sometimes blatantly unkind ways members of cliques treat outsiders. The positive side of such groups, however, is that they provide a way for adolescents to gain acceptance, support, and status outside the family.

Crowds typically consist of a number of cliques. Their function is different, with the emphasis being on social and recreational activities. Not surprisingly, crowds usually convene on weekends and can provide the basis for gatherings such as parties.

Much larger groupings also exist that have a looser structure and less well-defined membership. One high school was studied in which four major groupings emerged: jocks, motorheads, brains, and chewers. The first three are self-explanatory. In case you're wondering about the chewers, they were the students who liked to watch, rather than play sports, listen to country music, call each other on CB radios, and chew tobacco—and could do all at the same time. Those not identified with any of the four were described as "in-betweeners."

In addition to providing a sense of belonging and status, investment in groups outside the family provides a way of gaining social skills. Teenagers learn how to talk to different people, form judgments about others, and establish themselves in a particular hierarchy. They may want to experiment with being a leader and can find more opportunity to do this in peer groups as opposed to their families. They learn about sexual relationships and begin exploring what they want in a partner, as well as gaining insight into what they have to offer a potential mate.

Finding the right group—and getting into it—can be hard work. Teenagers may temporarily join a group just to see how comfortable they are in it. They may move between cliques and crowds until they find the types of relationships and activities that are satisfying and enjoyable to them. This can take time and can be very frustrating if they don't feel they belong anywhere. In my early teens I recall trying out for the jocks; I may have lasted an afternoon. At that point I disliked school, so I didn't even apply to be a brain.

Research has also looked at the changes in the importance of group membership over the course of adolescence. The pressure to belong to cliques and crowds usually becomes strong in early adolescence and reaches its peak in the midteens. By the time they're approaching adulthood and presumably feel somewhat more confident about themselves, the groupings often become much looser. Rather than definite cliques and crowds, there's more likely to be a network of friends and acquaintances who tend to get together socially. This pattern of interacting is one that persists throughout adulthood.

Peer groups can exert a lot of influence on young people; there's a strong pressure to conform, and parents can become concerned that this pressure may be negative. It can be very worrying to realize you have far less control over their friendships than was once the case. After all, there was a time when you almost always knew where they were and with whom, as well as enjoying veto rights over party invitations and guest lists for sleepovers. Now they want many of their social activities to be well away from the home, and you realize there's a significant part of their lives from which you're excluded.

I've always taken some comfort from the studies that have looked at the criteria adolescents use for selecting friends. In the chapter on sexuality I discussed the research that examines this issue with reference to dating. When it comes to broader friendships, it seems that teenagers also place value on qualities I'm sure most of us would applaud. For example, in a study in which teenagers had a choice of over 500 personality characteristics to describe the ideal qualities for a friend, the four that were picked with the highest frequency were sincerity, honesty, understanding, and loyalty. That's a pretty good profile. Of course, adolescents may make poor choices at times, but most learn from such mistakes and continue to seek to establish the kind of friendships and group affiliations that will help them develop in positive ways.

A WORLD OF THEIR OWN

When I first met Andrea I shared her parents' view that she seemed depressed. She had little animation: there were few signs of any emotional reaction to what she or other people were saying during the interview. At home she also seemed to be very distant. Her mother, in particular, had noted how often Andrea would stay in her room alone. She would have preferred to eat meals on her own if this had been allowed, and she rarely expressed any interest in going out with the family.

It took quite some time to reach the point where Andrea would discuss more than superficial matters with me. As I began to know her, however, I came to appreciate there were at least two reasons for her apparent withdrawal. The first was in keeping with her parents' perspective: Andrea was feeling unhappy about several matters. In this respect, spending time on her own could be seen as a symptom of emotional problems. At the same time, her solitude had a practical and valuable purpose. It was allowing her to undertake some thoughtful and necessary self-analysis and problem solving. Her major problems were that she hadn't yet found ways to deal with her dislike of her teacher and that she wasn't very popular at school. She used much of her time alone trying to figure out why she was having these difficulties and planning what she might do about them. She brought her diary to one session. It was full of suggestions she had for herself—almost like blueprints for action. My role became to act as her planning consultant, and I saw no reason to discourage her from spending time alone. I also encouraged her parents to view it as working in her room rather than retreating.

From studies of how adolescents use their time we know they're alone for approximately a quarter of their waking hours. This is a quantum leap from the amount of time young children spend on their own. So what are they doing? Believe it or not, a major pursuit seems to be constructive thinking. I'm sure we can all remember times in our lives when we've been faced with more change than we anticipated or more uncertainty and confusion than we felt able to handle. For most people, taking time to reflect, analyze, and plan is automatic. If we don't do this, we can be faced with the negative consequences that often follow rash and impulsive decisions. Adolescents are in much the same position, and probably even more so because of being in a period of very rapid and far-reaching change. They need to explore different ways of thinking and behaving. As one developmental psychologist, Paul Mussen, put it: "Adolescents need time to integrate the rapid changes occurring in their bodies and minds into a unified sense of identity." It sounds like heavy work, and it is.

When teenagers get behind closed doors, there's a chance they may actually be working, although I admit it's hard to know. Someone lying on a bed with a glazed expression might be in the throes of an existential dilemma, but they could also be goofing off. I suspect most adolescents indulge in both extremes, as well as many points in between. For the most part, however, I recommend that parents give their teenagers the benefit of the doubt. Unless there are indications of problems, such as depression, the need for solitude can be seen as healthy rather than as a sign that something is wrong or that parents and other family members are being rejected.

Regardless of what teenagers may actually be thinking when they're on their own, just having a physical space or territory that is theirs can help establish a degree of independence. We make great use of territory in our society. Having your own office, for example, is often a sign of having reached a certain status. And the more status you have, the bigger your office. This doesn't have to make any sense from the functional perspective. Bosses and supervisors rarely need a larger work area than their subordinates, but you'd be surprised if you found the president of a company in a small office.

Having their own space can be equally as important for adolescents, and the bedroom is the most likely territory. I had to share a room with my brother for many years. John was always far more organized than me, and he laid out clear guidelines and regulations regarding which areas were his and which were mine. He was older, wiser, and stronger—the perfect combination for giving him an edge in the negotiations regarding how to divide the territory. I recall that I was allotted a corner of the room that barely accommodated my bed and dresser; he generously added a thin track that allowed a path to the door. But this territory was *mine* and I was happy. We eventually moved and I had my own room. I can still remember how excited I was to have a space that was just my own. A declaration of independence quickly followed; I wanted no one else to enter my territory unless they had my permission. This declaration wasn't met with any resistance. While I believe I was always loved, nobody in the family was overwhelmed by grief or loneliness when I took myself off to my room, closed the door loudly, and did my own thing.

Just as a bedroom can become a symbol of adolescent independence, it can also become a battleground. I've heard countless horror stories over the years. One family was almost reduced to eating straight out of the cooking pots until they discovered that their son had full table settings for at least a dozen people hidden in various piles of papers and clothes in his bedroom. The daughter who literally couldn't remember the color of her bedroom carpet will also never be forgotten.

I've always been reluctant to become involved in the Battle of the Bedroom. Without wanting to go overboard in analyzing the symbolism, some teenagers use the bedroom as a means of asserting their need to make their own decisions and rules. From this perspective, not adopting house rules about neatness and cleanliness is a relatively harmless way of establishing a degree of independence from the family. Whenever my opinion is asked for, I recommend one of those hydraulic hinges that ensures the door is always shut (to be bought by the teenager in question). I also suggest the parents no longer take any responsibility whatsoever for their son's or daughter's laundry. If they'd rather throw a clean item of clothing in the general vicinity of the laundry basket than take the trouble to put it away for future use, let them rewash it. If they have no clean shirt or blouse for the school concert or have nothing to wear for the party, the old standby "tell someone who cares" may not exude empathy, but it covers all that needs to be said. They can have their privacy and establish a territory all their own; they can also have full responsibility for the consequences of not managing their territory efficiently.

REVISITING THE GENERATION GAP

Pushing away doesn't typically represent a real rejection of parents. It's more likely to be a phase in which teenagers take what they've learned from the family and begin applying it to the world in which they'll soon have to be independent. The notion of a significant gap between parents' and teenagers' values was challenged in Chapter Two. Teens are increasingly oriented toward their peers, but this isn't necessarily accompanied by a denunciation of adult values. When choices have long-term implications, teenagers are particularly likely to give more weight to the views of parents than to those of their peers. Parental style also has an important role to play here. When a more democratic style has been adopted, parents usually retain greater influence over their teenagers' decisions during adolescence. One study of mothers and daughters, for example, found that mothers were more likely to be seen as role models by their daughters if they weren't perceived as being rigid and authoritarian.

None of the above means your teenager will be sitting at your feet waiting for those pearls. But chances are they already know your views on most topics and could recite many of them word for word. Also, they've lived with you for many years and see your values reflected in your day-to-day actions. They can't help but know how much importance you place on ideals such as commitment to work and loyalty to family, equality of the genders, and moral obligation to help the disadvantaged. You've reached the stage in your relationship when you can begin to plan your retirement as a teacher; they've reached the stage in their development when there's far less need to seek or receive your opinions.

LETTING GO

While most of us don't find that our lives become meaningless after our adolescents have flown the nest, the process of separating isn't always easy for us. A teenager's task is to move away; ours is to let go, and this can be every bit as hard as theirs. In many ways the depth of our attachment to our children is unique and is hard for them to understand. They were almost totally dependent on us for many years, and we've felt a sense of caring and responsibility for them that they'll probably not experience until they become parents themselves.

I can remember becoming aware that our first two teenagers were no longer discussing certain areas of their lives with me. Every once in a while I'd suggest that if they didn't want me to know what was really happening in their lives, they could at least make something up so I'd feel informed. I also let them know that if they wanted me to feel really happy, they could invent a problem, seek my advice, and pretend to be impressed by my wisdom. Kiera and Aaron are following in their older siblings' footsteps and, while I understand the need for them to become more self-sufficient, I have to work hard to remind myself that they were loaned rather than given to me. Alexandra will be the last to leave, and after over three decades of living with children I know it will take time to adjust to the empty nest.

Sometimes the strength of the attachment parents have to their children can be matched by the strength of their resistance to recognizing the need to let go. The signs of this resistance are often easy to detect. I've seen many a teenager wince and sigh when their parents refer to themselves or each other as "mommy" and "daddy." They may be equally put out by kindly smiles in response to their views and complaints. To the adolescent this can be reminiscent of the amusement young children's comments and ideas often evoke. Of course, teenagers can contribute equally to the problem. Just as being treated as a 12-year-old when you're 15 can create conflict, so can trying to act like an 18-year-old. But for now I'm picking on us parents. We need to give our teenagers the opportunity to move away and try things out for themselves. They'll reach the stage when they have the right to make their own mistakes: this was a right our older children have exercised liberally.

Tim had a way with cars. He passed his driver's test shortly after his 16th birthday. It was his first attempt. Nothing to do with talent I assure you: the examiner who took him through his paces simply wanted to ensure the experience would never be repeated. It took Tim at least three years before he realized that a motor vehicle was a potentially dangerous machine and should be treated with more respect than a bumper car at the fairground. Don't misunderstand me, we were intent and serious in our efforts to instill in him a healthy respect for the automobile. As he'd heard more times than he cared to remember, I've had more opportunity than many people to see the tragic effects of car accidents. But there always comes a time when you have to stand aside, cross your fingers, and worry while your son or daughter begins to learn first-hand the lessons you wish they could learn directly from you. So Tim was allowed to drive the car.

Tim left the late movie one night and decided to take a shortcut from the parking lot to the main road home. He set off only to find that what he thought was a small lane was a footpath. This footpath disappeared, leaving Tim driving over wasteland. Always an astute and insightful person, he realized he'd be in trouble if the police noticed him, so he proceeded to turn his lights off. Not a bad move to avoid detection, but chances were also pretty good that Tim wouldn't spot anything either, such as the rather large boulder that did things to the underside of the car and allowed our mechanic to discharge his second mortgage.

What can you do? You can get mad. You can remove driving privileges. You can insist that your daughter or son pay for the damage. You can lecture. We did all of those things. But eventually we let him drive again. We didn't make him wait very long either. Our decision was that we'd prefer him to have the opportunity to learn how to drive responsibly as soon as possible. In many respects it was no different from the anxiety we'd experienced when he rode his bike. I swear children think they're immortal. I wish they never had to do anything even remotely dangerous. I wish we never had to sit at home and worry while they test their wings. We worry both because we love them and because we know they can get hurt— sometimes badly. So we do our best to prepare them. The rest is up to them, just as it was for us in our day.

TEST YOURSELF: THE LETTING GO QUIZ

Psychologists have a weakness for questionnaires. You name it and one of us has invented a scale to measure it. Romantic love, quality of life, and even fear of fat have been reduced to one of those pencil-and-paper, fill-it-out, and find-the-truth-about-yourself-in-under-three-minutes quizzes. Here's my contribution to the field of psychological testing; just by answering these questions you can discover if you're in need of major surgery to separate from your offspring.

1. I liked living with my child when she was 9. I will like it four times as much when she's 36.
2. Children who leave home before they're 40 are impulsive and rebellious.
3. I believe it's my responsibility to support my child until he's eligible for a pension.

4. Peter Pan is an ideal role model for children.
5. My child would be as the proverbial lost sheep without my guidance.
6. Having a child and receiving a life sentence are one and the same.
7. There's no one else to shovel the driveway and mow the lawn.
8. If my child left home she'd eat nothing but macaroni and die of scurvy.
9. My child has to stay at home to meet my need to be punished.
10. My life would be empty without the hassle, aggravation, and poverty that caring for my children brings.

If your true score is under 3, you're well on your way to enjoying the empty nest. Between 3 and 5 suggests you could have a struggle; every once in a while you'll probably throw a wet towel on the floor, cover the kitchen counter with crumbs, and leave all the lights on just to remind you of the old days. Anything over 5 is hopeless; you might as well resign yourself to terminal parenthood and begin negotiating what kind of curfews and limits will be appropriate for a 40-year-old.

THE GENTLE SHOVE

But what if you're ready to let them go and you can't get rid of them? Tracey was a 19-year-old who was in urgent need of leaving the nest, and I take some pride in knowing that I had a hand in her launching. She didn't enjoy living at home, and the lack of pleasure was mutual. Her parents commented and complained about the incredible transformation that seemed to take place as she walked up the driveway. In the community she acted like an adult, but by the time she was through the front door she seemed to have regressed to her early adolescence. Her parents couldn't understand how she could act so responsibly at work and still need to be reminded about the expectations and routines that had been established in the home for years. The amount of room and board to be paid was hardly more than nominal, but Tracey seemed to be viewing it as extortion. She argued that she needed to save as much as possible in case she decided to go to college, although her lifestyle suggested her savings account was in a sorry condition.

I don't want to paint too negative a picture. Tracey appeared to be a friendly, warm, and capable young woman. It was just that she needed to move on and hadn't. Her parents had considered the idea of telling her to leave, but it hadn't led to any action. Their concern was that Tracey would feel rejected, and they felt guilty at just the prospect of insisting that she spread her wings.

I've learned that you can't stop parents from feeling guilty. They are the world's leading authorities on the subject. They can blame themselves for anything and everything, and their favorite question is "where did we go wrong?" Having come to accept that parents need a certain amount of guilt, I try to capitalize on this emotion rather than fight it. So I suggested to Tracey that she sue her parents and that it would only be fair if they give her the money to do so. (I have to admit I like getting people's attention, and this worked very well.) The reason for the lawsuit was very simple. Tracey's parents had failed to provide the necessities of life. They were teaching her to be dependent and were robbing her of the opportunity to gain self-confidence and self-respect. She'd never learn how to manage a realistic budget or run her own household. As a result of her parents' neglecting her needs, she'd soon be brainwashed into believing she couldn't cope with the adult world on her own.

Tongue-in-cheek ideas can sometimes have an impact, and we subsequently spent several sessions debating the notion of whether or not it would be an act of kindness, as well as self-preservation, for the parents to insist she leave home. Tracey was obviously hesitant about this prospect; the predictability and comfort of home life can become addictive. But eventually a plan was made. A date for the launching was set, and her parents decided to make this a special occasion—a true celebration of her moving on. When I met with the family later I was pleased to hear that Tracey had at least made some effort to make her parents feel like "schmucks" for "kicking her out." It just doesn't feel right when teenagers go along with their parents without mounting some resistance.

This story does have a happy ending. The last session was just after the first dinner Tracey had cooked for her parents in her home. I'm sure the evening will be remembered as a signal of their new adult-to-adult relationship. Her parents even did the dishes without being told.

THE BOOMERANG GENERATION

Allow me a moment or two to vent. I have a strong aversion to anyone telling the rest of us what we should do, especially when it comes to family life. For example, there are times when stay-at-home parents are placed on a pedestal and compared to mothers who have abandoned their children by remaining in the competitive work force. Yet mothers who go against the trend by choosing to be full time homemakers can face the comment, "Oh, you're not working?" (Which roughly translates to: "So all you do is sit around all day watching the soaps while the rest of us keep the economy going.") Given my belief that, within reasonable bounds, families should be left to manage their own affairs, I'm not fond of the term "boomerang generation." It conjures up images of young adults who had too much of the good life when they lived with mom and dad. Unable to survive on their own without an SUV, designer clothes, and the prospect of an annual trip to the Caribbean, they head back to the nest. Unsuspecting parents welcome them, assuming it's just another short visit motivated by their offspring's love and wish to get their laundry done for free. Before they know what's hit them, their daughter has become a squatter—she's not going anywhere. What's more, she's reverted to adolescence. The nest is no more clean and tidy than it is empty, and your chances of being lonely in your old age are rapidly declining. But at least you'll have plenty to do. She'll need to be fed, and that laundry basket she brought with her seems to be refilled as soon as it's emptied.

I have to acknowledge the notion of a boomerang generation receives support from the statistics. The number of young adults living with their parents has increased substantially over the past two decades and now stands at just over 40 percent. Going to college or university is also becoming more of a temporary leave of absence than a step toward independence; slightly more than half of college students anticipate living back at home for a while after they graduate.

The trend, however, isn't necessarily an indication that young adults haven't got what it takes to survive out there in the big world, while their parents have become a soft-hearted lot who are all too willing to keep their doors and their wallets permanently open. The world has changed and adult life is less predictable. Young adults can expect to change their jobs more frequently than their parents did and they marry later in their lives. Obtaining a postsecondary education and training can also take many paths. Rising tuition fees can leave graduates with large debts that are hard to pay off when they haven't yet found secure, well-paid employment. Some may return home partway through their education or training and take advantage of the fact that the Internet allows them to complete their remaining credits through online courses.

Returning home may be an excellent decision for adult children, and one that meets with everyone's approval. While it's true some adult children rediscover some of the less endearing qualities of their adolescence, others return as fully mature people who share the responsibilities for maintaining the home. They take on chores without being nagged or even asked, they take their turn cooking meals, and they pay room and board. Their financial contribution may be particularly welcome in certain families—for example, when a parent can no longer work or is laid off.

Problems can arise and there are a few factors that are worth considering in order to avoid common pitfalls.

- **Establish financial arrangements up front.** One of the more common sources of tension relates to money—namely the adult child's willingness to spend his parents' money, but not his own, when it comes to day-to-day living expenses. Approximately 50 percent pay no rent, which can become a sore spot for parents. It seems not only unfair but can also interfere with the parents' lifestyle by reducing their disposable income.

You might wonder why so many parents don't negotiate finances before their daughter or son returns home. One obstacle is that parents have always provided the family home. The children didn't "stay" there—they were an essential part of what made it a home in the first place. Parents took care of all their children's needs, and although the thought may have crossed their minds at times, they didn't keep a running tab of all the child-rearing expenses in the hope of eventually recovering the costs. Given this history, putting a price on living back at home can seem hard-hearted and cold.

My advice is to recognize that being hard-hearted is an invaluable parenting skill at times. Give it a trial run, and I guarantee you'll agree. When they were younger they had no choice but to be dependent on you; that's one of the reasons we call them "children" and have special laws to protect them. But you had the responsibility to raise them to become "adults." The Merriam-Webster definition of an adult is someone who is "fully developed and mature." Fully developed and mature people pay their way whenever possible, and not charging them rent or room and board stunts their growth. Allowing them to hand over some of their money to you on a regular basis, therefore, enhances their growth and should be viewed as an act of caring and kindness.

Flexibility may be needed. The daughter returning home with very little money may not be able to make any financial contribution until she finds work. Parents may also decide to charge a relatively low amount if their son is working hard to save for a down payment on his own home. What can remain rigid, however, is the expectation that the adult child has to take on part of the financial responsibility for running the home.

- **Negotiate household responsibilities.** Unless you have a weakness for waiting on people hand and foot, sharing household tasks is a must. It can also be a plus. Imagine coming home two nights a week to your son's home cooking. Take the fantasy one step further: imagine his repertoire has expanded beyond hot dogs and grilled cheese sandwiches. While I'm on a roll, picture him cleaning the bathroom on the weekend after doing the grocery shopping. Share this fantasy with him, stressing the need for him to turn it into a reality.

- **Avoid shelving your own plans.** It can be a mistake for parents to abandon their own plans when one of their children returns home. This is particularly true for empty nesters. The ability to adjust to change is an essential part of human development. I've watched friends who have been genuinely sad and even distraught when their children have left home become enthusiastic about the new lifestyle associated with fewer responsibilities and expenses.

  I encourage parents to keep a tight rein on any impulse they might have to come out of retirement and focus their attention on their children. Once they've adopted "cold-hearted" as a parenting skill, this isn't too much of a challenge. In most situations, there's little reason why the parents should change their new-found lifestyle. Areas of the house may have been redesigned on the basis of the parents' interests. A room that once functioned as an at-home video arcade and movie theater may now be an exercise room or art studio. Timing and content of meals often change when there are no children at home; parents may also eat more of their meals with friends, either at home or out. None of the foregoing need change, and the expectation can be that the returning child works around her parents' new lifestyle whenever this is possible.

- **Have a clear plan regarding the future.** On occasion, returning home may be a long-term arrangement. If parents and their adult children want to establish a permanent household together, that's obviously their right, and there's no need for a psychologist to comment beyond wishing them all the best. But in most situations returning home is viewed as temporary—a step on the way to full independence. Trouble arises, however, when the definition of "temporary" isn't clarified. Parents can be concerned that asking the question, "And how long do you want to live at home?" sounds too much like, "If you must come home, at least give us something to look forward to." But, again, it really is for their own good to have an exit plan. The goal may be to find a job and save enough for first and last on an apartment. In this case, the arrangement is seen as very short-term. A longer stay would be necessary if the plan is to finish the last years of a degree program from home.

The plan can go beyond determining the exit date. Young adults may have had difficulty with money management, and part of the plan can be that parents will help them learn how to budget more efficiently and save the funds they'll need to move out.

- **Above all, talk to one another.** Living together as adults can't be the same as living together as parents and children. Open discussion is an acknowledgement that family members need to work together to make the plan successful. The old model of family life that existed throughout childhood no longer applies.

The research is encouraging. While there are families in which returning children lead to parental dissatisfaction, these are a minority. Related research has also documented the extent to which the adult children and their parents receive emotional support from one another. An interesting finding was that the parents said they received more emotional support than their children realized they had given. Sometimes just living under the same roof, regardless of the level of interaction, can give the support we need.

CHAPTER 14

WHO ARE THE EXPERTS?

Several years ago I began browsing in second-hand bookstores. I forget why I developed this pastime, but I inevitably found myself drawn to the titles relating to my field. Soon I had a modest collection of long-forgotten books about child-rearing. Outmoded as they were, they taught me a valuable lesson: I became acutely aware of how easy it can be for people with professional qualifications to believe they're truly experts. I read books by authors who were understandably seen as prominent members of their professions. They had graduated from established universities, held responsible positions, and were obviously highly respected members of society. Yet many of the beliefs they held and much of the advice they offered would be seen by most of us today as nothing short of ridiculous. They weren't frauds or quacks bent on deceiving the populace for personal gain. They were sincere and well-meaning people who had the best interests of children in mind when they wrote. To illustrate my point I'd like to return to the Victorian era and present a few examples of what the experts were saying.

STORKS, GOOSEBERRY BUSHES, AND OTHER FABLES

I can't remember when I first asked about how I came into this world. I suppose that at some tender age I expressed an interest in how I'd happened to appear. I do recall that my brother had a burning desire to find out how I'd arrived, but only because of his wish to send me back.

I also can't remember what type of reply I typically received when inquiring about baby-making. Like many of my generation, I recall having heard about storks and finding babies under gooseberry bushes. Perhaps we once believed these fables, but they did no permanent damage. Telling young children that they came by airmail may be a trifle silly, but is it any more outrageous than trying to convince them that a large man loves children so much he squeezes down millions of chimneys in a single night to give them presents, or that a rabbit hops around the world leaving jelly beans and chocolate eggs?

One hundred years ago the experts would have vehemently attacked the indifference I've expressed about such fables. I'm not talking about an honest disagreement or a lively debate as to whether or not children should be given the truth rather than a fairy story. The experts would have seen me as a very dangerous person, someone who should never be allowed to publish his views.

The Victorians fascinate me. They had a certain passion we seem to lack. Once they believed something they were unshakable. Because of grave concerns about lying, one prominent physician and writer began contemplating how this characteristic might develop. First of all she used the cardinal rule that mothers are the best targets whenever an expert wants to lay blame. (In case you didn't know, they have single-handedly caused schizophrenia, autism and, I suspect, athlete's foot and the hole in the ozone layer.) So it came as no surprise to learn that mothers cause the problem, or to quote: "Nearly everyone who is now grown up got his (or her) first lesson in lying at his mother's knee." And what might this lesson be? Storks and gooseberry bushes, of course. Such myths penetrate the subconscious and the child "receives a mental warp and injury which nothing can ever eradicate entirely." You can try to make it up to them, but no number of anatomy and physiology lessons or diagrams of the reproductive system can undo the damage you've caused.

Let's say that you were a wise and knowledgeable parent who'd never made mention of storks or gooseberry bushes. But did you teach them nursery rhymes? Another expert was ready to pounce on you. This time the problem wasn't that you were giving them false information. (After all, dishes don't elope with spoons and the chances of blackbirds singing after being baked in a pie are pretty remote.) What you'd be doing, however, is stunting their growth. "How?" you might ask. Simple. Memorizing nursery rhymes sends too much blood to the brain and diverts the "nerve-force" from its primary duty of organizing physical growth. Overtaxing the mind in this way guarantees that harmful effects will follow. So if your son or daughter is below average height, take a hard look at yourself. How many times did you sit down together with the Mother Goose books? Was it really worth it? Any chance of ever making the basketball team was wiped out just because you thought it was cute to have them recite Humpty Dumpty for grandma.

The level of guilt and fear generated in parents must have been high. If you were one of those parents who'd overtaxed your child's brain, the prospects weren't good. You read on to learn that "if the life of the child be spared, the future is liable to be blighted by a general want of strength and by disorders caused by a defective nerve-force."

Before leaving the Victorians I want to go back to the topic of legs. It wasn't until I read Dr. Rankin's *Hygiene of Childhood* (1890) that I understood covering legs was more than just a reflection of modesty. Cold feet meant increased blood flow to the higher regions of the body and hence greater risk of pelvic congestion. This, in turn, it was stated, created a risk of inflammation and death. The habit of wearing only slippers in the house was, therefore, extremely hazardous to health. Insisting that daughters wear shoes, woolly socks, and flannel drawers was seen as nothing less than a life and death issue.

It's easy to be critical when you have access to an extra century's worth of information. I can look back at the sixties and recall that the mini-skirt and bikini didn't wipe out most of the female population as Dr. Rankin would surely have predicted. My criticism of the Victorian authorities on child-rearing, however, isn't that they were wrong; it's that they acted as if they had exclusive access to the truth. They claimed they were simply passing on the laws of nature that parents would disregard at their children's peril. They rarely offered their statements as views, opinions, or theories: they knew the truth and the rest of us better listen. Our duty was to understand the laws of health they were presenting, recognizing that we were almost always responsible for the physical and mental pain and misery that might fall upon our offspring.

HAVE THINGS CHANGED?

At times it seems the claims being made by modern-day experts are just as outrageous as those of their Victorian ancestors. Recent assertions that parents are virtually irrelevant in their children's lives because of the overriding influence of genetic inheritance and peers provide a topical example. In this respect the myth that truth has been discovered is revised. Most people in the childcare field, however, tend to be far less dogmatic than their predecessors. There's more discussion of "approaches" and less insistence that the ideas being offered are laws of nature.

When I was studying experimental psychology, I recall being advised that social scientists should be ambitious and bold in what they attempt, but modest in what they claim. I like to keep this advice in mind whenever I consider the field of child psychology—and, in particular, child-rearing. Conducting research that's valid and relevant is so hard to do. All of us would love to know the best way to raise our children so they grow up to be well-adjusted members of society. But could we ever agree on how to define a term such as "well-adjusted" in the first place? Just how should success be measured when it comes to being a parent? Is it in terms of academic or vocational achievement? If so, what's the best way to measure achievement? With respect to academic success, is it just the level of qualification that matters? But what about effort and motivation? Do we want to think of a young person who worked very hard to reach grade 12 as less successful than a gifted student who coasted through college with mediocre marks? And what about success in the working world? What are the measures to use? Salary level? Number of employees under your control? Contribution of the work to society?

You might decide to focus more on children's personality and emotional development. Immediately the problems with definition resurface. What are the important personality characteristics? Does being a warm, sociable person count more or less than being an assertive individual with leadership qualities? What is more worthwhile: feeling a strong need to achieve or having a content and relaxed attitude toward life?

One last problem has to be mentioned. Even if we could agree on how to measure children's success or adjustment, it would be very difficult to know for sure what actually caused them. The way parents treat their children undoubtedly has a major influence on their development, but so do many other factors, such as heredity, school, peer groups, and the prevailing culture. Trying to untangle all these effects and determine how much impact each has on the way we are as children and adults has always been a major headache for social scientists. Given the readiness with which the experts have responded to children's problems by convicting parents without even considering other potential culprits, I feel obliged to make a contribution to correcting the imbalance. I accept full responsibility only for those things my children do that could be seen as success-ful; all else is the result of the combined influences of their mother's genetic legacy, the alignment of the stars at their birth, and their kindergarten teachers.

To my mind, the state of our knowledge is far from the point where anyone in my field can come close to being able to present themselves as experts who hold the key to successful parenting. At best, we can act as consultants to families and can justify offering this service on two counts. The first is that, because we spend much of our daily lives talking to children and parents, we hear a lot about the issues that create conflict and about the steps families are taking to try to make things better. As we offer suggestions and listen to theirs, we learn which ones tend to work and which ones aren't so useful. In other words, we learn from the experiences of working with families in the same way that all adults learn from carrying out their daily responsibilities.

The second reason for believing we should still be allowed to practice in spite of my insistence there are no real experts is that we should be keeping ourselves familiar with the studies conducted in the field. While I may have poked fun at research (including my own), I do hope that social scientists will continue to get their grants and will add to our understanding of human behavior. I personally find their results helpful. I've been impressed enough by the research into parenting styles that there's no way our youngest children will be given the opportunity to have the freedom their older brother and sister enjoyed. I'm also convinced I worked too hard teaching values to my teenagers. Chances are that, for better or worse, we've laid the foundation of our children's moral and social thinking by the time they reach adolescence. Chances are also good that, whether or not they actually talk to us about their major decisions, they do attach weight to our opinions. So while Aaron, Kiera, and Alexandra were denied the experience of going to school wearing swimsuits over their clothes, they were spared most of my standard, overused lectures.

I encourage parents to seek ideas and suggestions. I'd never, of course, discourage them from buying books about teenagers; there are even some suggestions at the back of this book as to which ones they might purchase. The self-help sections of bookstores have grown in size and contain many titles on child-rearing. There are also audiotapes and videotapes that discuss topics such as communication, discipline, and sexuality. Community groups sponsor speakers and workshops to increase our parenting skills and phone-in shows offer advice for specific problems. To top it all off, you may have the benefit of your own parents who will, at no cost, provide a regular report card and summary of what you should be doing. Before I get in deep trouble, I want to state publicly that I always appreciated my mother's approach. She argued that if she'd been an effective model of how to be a parent, we'd follow suit and she'd have no reason to intervene. On the other hand, if she hadn't done such a good job, she'd be the last person who should give advice to the next generation of parents. Either way, we could count on her respecting us as parents.

Having listened to all the advice—invited and otherwise—parents will always be left with the most critical step. Only they have the knowledge that's needed to decide what particular action will best meet the needs of their daughter or son in a given situation. Research and theories in the social sciences can never take full account of the vast range of individual differences among children and young people; that requires a depth of understanding and sensitivity that comes only through years of sharing your life with someone. Parents may not often feel like experts, but sometimes the people most qualified for a job are the last to know it.

ACKNOWLEDGEMENTS

There's a certain irony to the fact that writing about family life has meant I neglected my own. My wife, Kathy, rarely complained about my absences and even insisted I not emerge from my study before completing the next section of the manuscript.

Revising this book has given me the pleasure of working with Elaine Jones again, as well as Ben D'Andrea. Editors like Elaine and Ben are wonderful people; they make all kinds of improvements to a book but allow the author to get the credit.

Each edition of this book reminds me of the encouragement and support I received from Lorraine Greey. She introduced me to Whitecap and was instrumental in launching my writing career. All she ever asked for was a copy of the book.

I've always admired Barbara Coloroso's ability to talk to her audiences and readers in such a clear, instructive, and compassionate manner. Her influence and advice were invaluable to me when I began speaking, and she has kindly provided the foreword for this book.

Thank you.

RESOURCES

BOOKS AND TAPES

Chapman, Gary. *The Five Love Languages of Teenagers.* Chicago: Moody Press, 2001.

Coloroso, Barbara. *kids are worth it! Giving Your Child the Gift of Inner Discipline.* Toronto: Penguin Books of Canada, 2000.

———. *Winning at Parenting* (tapes): www.kidsareworthit.com.

Engber, Andrea. *The Complete Single Mother: Reassuring Answers to Most Challenging Concerns.* Cincinnati: Adams Media Corporation, 2006.

Giron, Amy, and Charles Miron. *How to Talk with Teens About Love, Relationships, and S-E-X: A Guide for Parents.* Minneapolis: Free Spirit Publishing, 2002.

Mitchell, Barbara. *The Boomerang Age: Transitions to Adulthood in Families.* Somerset: Transaction Publishers, 2005.

Nelson, Jane. *Positive Discipline for Single Parents: Nurturing Cooperation, Respect, and Joy in Your Single-Parent Family.* Rocklin: Prima, 1999.

Roddel, Victoria. *Internet Safety Family Guide.* Lulu Enterprises: Morrisville, NC: 2005.

Dr. Marshall's previous books—*Cinderella Revisited: How to Survive Your Stepfamily Without a Fairy Godmother* and *Sex, Nursery Rhymes and Other Evils: A Look at the Bizarre, Amusing, Sometimes Shocking Advice of Victorian Childcare Experts*—can be obtained directly from the author (www.petermarshall.com). His book *Two Jobs, No Life: Learning to Balance Work and Home* is available from Key Porter Books.

INTERNET SITES

These sites offer a broad range of information about children of all ages.

www.familyeducation.com

www.media-awareness.ca
(information for parents and children about the media, including the Internet)

www.parentsoup.com

www.singleparents.org
(Single Parents Association)

www.stepfamilies.info
(Stepfamily Association of America and National Stepfamily Resource Center)

www.todaysparent.com

www.wiredkids.org
(an upbeat approach to basic Internet protection; downloadable booklet at www.wiredkids.org/ parents/parentingonline)

INDEX

ABOUT THE AUTHOR

Born in England, Dr. Marshall has lived in Canada since 1973. He is the father of five and has worked for over 25 years as a practising clinician and university professor. He is also an international speaker and has appeared on numerous television and radio programs to discuss current issues relating to family life. His previous books are *Cinderella Revisited: How to Survive Your Stepfamily Without a Fairy Godmother, Two Jobs, No Life: Learning How to Balance Work and Home*, and *Sex, Nursery Rhymes and Other Evils: A Look at the Bizarre, Amusing, Sometimes Shocking Advice of Victorian Childcare Experts*. He lives in Barrie, Ontario, with his family.